BOOK ENDS:
A year between the covers

Books by Naomi Beth Wakan

*Compositions: Notes on the written word*

*Haiku: One Breath Poetry*

*Late Bloomer: On Writing Later in Life*

*Segues*

# BOOK ENDS
## A year between the covers

Naomi Beth Wakan

POPLAR
**PRESS**

Published in Canada by Poplar Press, a division of Wolsak and Wynn Publishers Ltd., Hamilton.

Cover image: Eli Wakan
Cover design: Julie McNeill
Author's photograph: Eli Wakan
Sculptor credit: *Naomi Beth Wakan* by Nancy Crozier
Typeset in Leawood
Printed by Ball Media, Brantford, Canada

The publishers gratefully acknowledge the support of the Canada Council for the Arts, the Ontario Arts Council and the Book Publishing Industry Development Program (BPIDP) for their financial assistance.

The Canada Council | Le Conseil des Arts
for the Arts | du Canada

ONTARIO ARTS COUNCIL
CONSEIL DES ARTS DE L'ONTARIO

Canadian       Patrimoine
Heritage       canadien

Poplar Press.
69 Hughson Street North, Ste. 102
Hamilton, ON
Canada L8R 1G5
www.wolsakandwynn.ca

**Library and Archives Canada Cataloguing in Publication**

Wakan, Naomi
    Book ends : a year between the covers / Naomi Beth Wakan.

ISBN 978-1-894987-42-4

I. Title.
PS8595.A547Z462 2010        C814'.54        C2010-900117-6

To Alberto Manguel
– a model writer, and reader

# Contents

# Introduction

It was a blustery winter's day as I recorded the last of my literary reflections for the year, when suddenly the power went out on our little island of Gabriola. As trees are shallow-rooted on this rock-pile, they frequently are persuaded by the visiting breezes to fall on power lines and subsequently cause power outages.

With my computer now useless, I sighed briefly, picked up the closest book to hand and settled into the cushions on the window seat, covered myself with an afghan and snuggled in for a guilt-free afternoon's read. The book I had picked up was *Walden* by David Thoreau, a book often quoted from, but rarely read (at least by anyone that I know). I myself (as I mention in my August entry) had resisted it for over thirty years, thinking Thoreau overly opinionated (and this based only on hearsay). First rule of book reading – don't be guided by other people's opinions. Within ten minutes I had been swept away and was sitting on the doorstep of Thoreau's little hut he had built for himself by Walden Pond, listening eagerly to his arguments as to why we should "simplify, simplify" and why we should be more aware of the way we live.

I had set out on a journey and had become enchanted. That is what it is like every time I pick up a book. Sometimes I hesitate at the doorstep, sometimes I plunge into dark, unknown places, sometimes I skirt the edge of madness, but always I return to our little vinyl-sided house on Gabriola Island with a nugget of information about the world, or about myself.

Imagine my delight when I discovered that Thoreau, with whom I had shared the afternoon, had a gem to share with readers also. "To read well, that is, to read true books in a true spirit, is a noble exercise, and one that will task the reader more than any exercise which the customs of the day esteem. It requires a training such as the athletes underwent, the steady intention of almost the whole life to this object."

*Book Ends* is ostensibly my reading record for a year, which I invite the reader to dip into and to note down books that they too might want to journey into. But more than that, I am tasking my reader to take their role very seriously, for the reader is the final contributor to the creation of a book. What they bring to a book, what they expect from a book will determine what they are able to extract. What the reader gleans from their reading may very well decide not just their own future, but the future of our planet, for books can swing people around, and people can bring about changes, small or large, to benefit us all.

In *Book Ends,* both you, the reader, and I stand centre stage in a role that extends our own lives backwards through the reading of times past, or forwards into possible scenarios. In turn, we extend the life of the book we are reading forwards by our very act of reading, and the possibility that our reading may stir us to action. The writer cannot manage without us and where would we be without the writer. Here's to us both!

# January

Usually we start the New Year with a certain quiet determination in our little vinyl-sided cottage on our small
island of Gabriola, but this year there seems to be an
unusual level of flurry and scurry. This curious amount of
activity is being caused by the fact that it has somehow
finally been determined that this is to be the year of a real
push towards a zero-mile diet on our property. We, my
husband Eli and I, tried this some years ago on five fertile
acres in Ontario, but fell somewhat short of our target, so
how we are going to achieve it now on a half-acre rock-pile
in BC is a mystery. Still, Eli loves puzzles and for the last
few months he has been happily running around the property measuring tree elevations around the horizons that
surround the garden and orchard; calculating the total
amount of possible annual sunshine at various spots on the
property; marking trees that, if cut down, would greatly
increase the hours of direct sunshine at one spot or
another; planning more deer-proof fencing and racoon-
control measures; and at the same time determining where
a cistern should be placed to gather the rainwater from the
roof. All this should have been finished last summer, or at
the latest by the fall, so I suspect Eli's stack of papers
impressively covered with charts of the angles of sun
obstructions, solar hours per day and weather statistics is

being produced to cover his enormous capacity for procrastination. It is so uncharacteristic of him to be making New Year's resolutions, particularly ones that are literally so down to earth.

The only New Year's resolutions I am choosing to make revolve around my book-box and so, with hopes high, I pick up the weighty copy of Thomas Mann's *Doctor Faustus* as my first reading of the year. I borrowed the book following the earnest suggestions of my intellectual friends that this is a "must-read." The initial pace of the book does not fit my New Year's mood, which is bright, chirpy and hopeful. I also don't hear the noise of a trap springing, which would indicate to me that I am truly caught up by this book, pulled in, a willing captive.

I am reluctant to put a book down without salvaging something from it though, and so I begin flipping through the pages. Has anyone before me dared to flip through *Doctor Faustus,* I wonder? I am quite taken with the phrase "the prickling sensation that came with realizing one was exposing to sight what had never been seen, was not to be seen, had never expected to be seen." This sentence describes the moment of artistic creation and it struck me hard, so that when, three hundred pages later, I found the very same words describing a trip to the seabed in a bathysphere, I immediately noted the repetition, as if Mann had plagiarized himself. Satisfied with this small discovery, I respectfully laid the book on the "return" shelf. For the next few weeks I duck behind parked cars when I see the folk, who had recommended *Doctor Faustus* to me, across our little shopping mall on our Saturday jaunts into the village. I hate to disappoint people.

**/ILⱭI\**

*Mega biblion, mega kakon,* "big book, big evil." This quote by Callimachus is from my next New Year's choice, Louis de Bernières' *Captain Corelli's Mandolin.* I should have picked it up before I attempted Dr. Faustus.

Metaxas in *Captain Corelli's Mandolin* says, "If I had lived my life in the consciousness of death, everything would have been different." Every day I wonder if this is to be my last day. People assume I do this because of my recent years with cancer, or, before that, my study of Buddhist meditation, but if I had to give this rather odd practice an origin it would be the moment I was pulled by forceps from my mother's body, having lingered within for two hours after my twin had emerged. I was probably sulking that she had managed to get out first, but anyway, I was nearly dead on arrival. Maybe I have watched *Grey's Anatomy* for one season too long, but in my imagination I picture the young interns of seventy-eight years ago, distracted from their amorous adventures by my pathetic birth, asking each other, "will she make it?" "Is she going to die?" So, for the rest of my life I continued asking myself the very same questions as they had, as they registered on my barely-formed little brain.

This daily practice of *momento mori,* however, does somehow make the day's activities more urgent, more precious. I do this every morning, just before I get up, irrespective of whether I feel like a sprightly sixteen years old or a decrepit ninety. My twin, after recent surgery, says she now feels "old" and I know what she means. Occasionally, say when walking down an icy slope, I feel as an old person might, and know that my seventy-eight years can allow me to feel that way.

Again from the Captain, "History is the propaganda of the victor." You must read this book, not just to hear of the horrors of the battlefront, but to hear of the botches of the dictators and their duplicity, and also to hear of small acts of loving and caring in the midst of Hell. I know these comments make it sound as though each book I read must have a utilitarian aspect, and that fiction, in a way, should be read as non-fiction. This is not entirely so, for often I read just for the pleasure of communicating with the author's mind and what he or she wants to tell me, in addition to my Puritanical desire to make the book useful – to milk a book for what will enrich my life. Louis de Bernières has lots to tell me and plenty that will benefit me in his fine book.

More quotes from the Captain, "Love is what is left over when being in love has burned away." And, "It's a moral principle that you can't alter, not a scientific fact." I ponder this one for a bit, and decide that while it is true that two plus two equalling four may have an element of doubt in it, does "killing is wrong" not likewise have times when it is not applicable? Moral principles also are not written in stone, I feel, notwithstanding the report of the Ten Commandments having such a solid base.

I could quote endlessly from this prodigious book, but here's a last thought for now, "Every man needs an obsession in order to enjoy life." Mine, I suppose, is reading. I continue to read obsessively, ever looking for a book that will tell me why there is something instead of nothing, in words I can understand, even though I suspect my journey is unlikely to be successful as long as I am trapped within three dimensions.

I often discuss reasons for reading with attendees at my workshops. We all have different reasons at various times, depending on our needs and our moods. I usually offer one of mine first, to prime the pump as it were. For example, at a workshop, I might choose to say that I read in order to enter another reality, so that in its exploration, perhaps I will find fresh perspectives that might help me deal with the bewildering reality I live in. Another time, I might offer that I pick up a book to feel creativity in my hand.

Their reasons for reading have included: the desire to get information on a subject, that reading presents a mirror for themselves, for the sheer joy of rollicking in carefully chosen words, in order to get totally absorbed in something outside themselves, to explore the geography of the human psyche, to escape, to recapture childhood memories, in order to calm down, and (no disrespect to the author) to help one fall asleep. But perhaps the simplest reason for obsessional reading is that it is an inherited addiction. The obsession is in the genes.

**ЛДІ\**

Today I am musing on having a patron, or perhaps a sugar daddy ... well "it's too late for that," my wrinkled skin tells me. This is brought on by dipping into an old favourite, Somerset Maugham's *Cakes and Ale,* where I read about a poet being picked up by a patron. The patron has luncheons to introduce the poet to the "right" people; makes parties where the poet reads his stuff before "distinguished" people; guides his poetry into the "right" journals and gets exaggerated contracts for him, finishing up by separating him from his wife, a thing with which, the patron feels, a serious artist should not be encumbered. When the poet fails to come up to snuff, the patron elegantly and quietly reverses the process, vowing to pick a winner next time around. I knew an artist once who had a patron while he was struggling to get recognition. When the artist eventually stood on his own two feet, however, the patron didn't like his own changed role and carefully listed how much money he had spent on buying the artist's works. So much for charity. When push comes to shove, charity is never a pretty sight to behold.

**/IL∠I\**

Why am I reading a history of England (a country I left so many years ago) written by a British art historian ensconced in an American university? Historians, it is said, like quiet lives. I recall that William Hickling Prescott (not the art history professor I refer to above) certainly had one, since his blindness limited his activities. Yet within his terrible limitations, he still managed to write several major histories. He employed a reader who read and reread, hundreds of texts aloud to him. Prescott could amazingly recall all this material and dictate pages of text with barely a moment's pause. I have his excellent *History of the Conquest of Peru* and *History of the Conquest of Mexico* on my bookshelves. By the way, before he started on his great histories, he taught himself Italian, Latin and French, and then added Spanish in order to spend seven years writing the history of Ferdinand and Isabella. For writing, he used a strange device called an octograph, a portfolio with brass guide wires to indicate the lines. His histories are still guiding writers today.

And speaking of writers overcoming inconceivably great odds, my greatest inspiration is Jean-Dominique Bauby, who wrote an entire book with his left eyelid, being completely paralysed except for that lid. Yes, please add *The Diving Bell and the Butterfly* to your list to remind you how limitations can be overcome.

On to Simon Schama's jaunty *A History of Britain 1: At the Edge of the World? 3000 BC – AD 1603,* which covers everything up to Elizabeth the first. What a mess of battles and gory bodies. I read that in 1290, England was the first country to expel Jews. Mr. Schama says, "it was as if they were a contagious disease." What a world to live in ... then, and still now.

Elsewhere in Schama's book, I am reminded that "the best things are those that are not long-looked-forward-to – the ones looked-forward-to are usually let-downs." It's in those small everyday moments, when perhaps an apt quote, come across by chance, hits home, that Heaven and Earth seem to knit together for a minute and one feels it is possible to continue on with this nonsense world.

# /ILᐊI\

I just spent the weekend reading Heather Mallick's two books of essays – *Pearls in Vinegar: The Pillow Book of Heather Mallick* and *Cake or Death: The Excruciating Choices of Everyday Life.* They are marvellous, and so is she. I write to tell her so, and include for her enjoyment my poem about Sei Shōnagon and those Japanese Heian court women and their diaries.

### Reprimand to Those Japanese Court Women

Oh you stupid court women!
Have you nothing better to do
than spend long nights crying
into your futon about how
you can still feel his hands
in your dishevelled hair,
still smell the lingering scent
of his clothes on your own.
Why, anything triggers your tears:
the call of a mountain cuckoo,
the quail crying out,
or the plover piping.
Your buckwheat pillow is soggy
and your *koto* is out of tune.
Can't you see the paths
to your house are overgrown
and deep in snow.
You must understand that the Gods
have decreed your northwesterly
direction forbidden to him
for the rest of the year,
and probably the rest of your life!
Your heart may be withering,
the skies filled with clouds,

and even the moon is slow and sinking,
yet gazing at your soaked pillow,
and trying to unknot your twisted strands
will not help matters at all.
Why don't you read Sei Shōnagon
and take matters into your own hands.
Start making lists, that will stop
the flow of your tears.
begin with "Depressing Things"
and get them out of your system.
Next things that "Should be short"
such as unrequited love.
Soon you'll be brushing your long hair
and grinding a load of fresh ink
in order to list
"Things that have lost their power."

I sent the poem because Heather uses the format of Sei Shōnagon's *Pillow Book* for her own books. A pillow book is a collection of quotes and observations reflecting the writer's life and the period they live in. For example, Sei Shōnagon's pillow book gave a wonderful and caustic description of court life in the Heian period in Japan. My poem above tells of the love poetry the court women wrote at that time – usually of unrequited love and cast-aside loneliness – whiny and endlessly mournful! Heather Mallick's books of essays have neither of these qualities. Her complaints are direct and forceful and Heather's comments are equally as caustic as Shōnagon's.

I receive a letter back from Ms. Mallick that indicated she had marked my website and would treasure my letter. I get a little buzz, for although I can never be Heather Mallick, her writing does give me a lesson in outspokenness, and "outspokenness" is the buzzword for my aspirations in my writing at the moment.

In her letter, she says she got into trouble for her essay on why she hates America. I am not surprised. In this essay in *Cake or Death,* while speaking of her feelings on the subject, she says, "When I meet someone who isn't anti-American, and I include Americans in this, I think they're either stupid or they've been busy with eighteen-month-old twins and haven't had time to think about it." She complains that Americans hold every other nation in contempt, even as their empire disintegrates, and wonders how adults can wear overalls, T-shirts and sneakers. (She rings a bell with me here, for I have wondered for some years how adult men can wear schoolboys' caps.) All the above comments are in her blistering essay, so please get the book and read it, for as she comments, "Millions of children starve because of Americans swelled up on this planet and nothing can be done."

I admire her ferocity enormously but since I don't see things quite so black and whitely as she does, I do have some suggestions about how matters in the world could be improved; simplistic they may be, but better than nothing when it comes to trying to get the world back in balance. For example, aid (often from America), that corrupt third-world dictators channel off into their own Swiss bank accounts, could be rerouted to the advantage of the starving populations they drain. A small offering, and unlikely to be taken up, for who has ever listened to me.

Some of my own anti-American tendencies stem from my university days when (even though I was only at a red-brick university built for the education of workers' offspring) we would scathingly say that you could get a degree in confectionary from any American University, with honours in licorice allsorts. We also had an American air-force base near the town in the north of England, to which our family had been evacuated during World War II, and I and my friends all knew the "bad" girls who fraternized with the "overpaid, oversexed and over-here" Yanks because "those girls" had to filter into the assembly after Christian prayers, for they would have just finished a morning detention. Unfortunately, we Jewish riff-raff also entered the main assembly along with the recalcitrant young women. In our case, we entered late because of our supposed faith, rather than our sexual tendencies. At fourteen, I already knew the world was unfair, but, as my mother-in-law has been quoted, "Who says the world has to be fair?"

Anyway Heather's essay finishes with the words "go to hell, America. I couldn't have dreamed of a more awful place if I'd tried." I have had some pleasant holidays in America, so I can't completely agree with her, although I am green with envy at her ability to express her feelings so succinctly.

ΛLΔΙ\

Having finished the two books by Heather Mallick, I realize how much I enjoy a good book of essays. This time I've picked up Margaret Atwood's *Curious Pursuits: Occasional Writing*. I am delighted to find here a "Letter to America" and so can compare her reactions to Heather's. Her letter is much softer; in fact, a mere warning, for there is much she loves about America. The warning is about descending down a slippery slope that will result in people's admiration being withdrawn. "They'll decide that your city upon the hill is a slum and your democracy a sham, and therefore you have no business trying to impose your sullied vision on them." I notice that the good things Ms. Atwood lists about America are mainly in the field of music, as are Heather's.

Ms. Atwood just doesn't have Heather's sparks. In spite of her impish asides I still see her in a girdle, white gloves and hose with their seams perfectly straight, her Anglo-Saxon slip just showing slightly at the bottom edge of her pleated skirt, as it does in all her writing. How could it not? I only laughed aloud once in the whole reading of her book, whereas with Heather's two books, my merry peals echoed throughout the house and bounced against our vinyl-siding. No. I don't see the world only as amusing. I see the world as absurd and often nightmarish, but the way I have chosen to deal with this is with laughter. It is so much more positive than gassing yourself like Sylvia Plath or walking into the water as did Virginia Woolf, the latter an author whom Atwood, Mallick and Anne Fadiman all seem to admire, as do I, though for her writing, rather than her manner of exit.

## ⑥

Speaking of Anne Fadiman, I find her book of essays, *Ex Libris: Confessions of a Common Reader,* is next in the pile on my garage-sale coffee table and lo and behold she too has an essay on America, on the American flag to be exact. "A Piece of Cotton," she modestly entitles it, so perhaps it will be an antidote to Mallick and Atwood's heavy negatives. We shall see.

Anne Fadiman is a middle-class girl with a famous father, Clifton Fadiman, and an incredibly encouraging upbringing including Harvard. She became editor of *The American Scholar* and is now writer-in-residence at Yale. Can one ask for anything more American? Not the trailer parks and malls perhaps, but let's see what she has to say about her stars and stripes.

She and her family decided to hang the flag at half-mast after 9/11. Her husband solemnly intones, "This flag is lowered now, but it will rise again, just as our country will." I don't know how he can be so sure of that, seeing that most folks I read think that his country is going to hell in a handbasket very fast. I have stopped counting at forty the number of countries the US has invaded in order to help spread democracy. Why over one hundred and fifty years ago Simon Bolivar, had already warned that "inviting the United States to the Congress of Panama is 'like inviting the cat to the mice's fiesta.'" "Don't go to the States," he warned, "it's omnipotent and terrible, and its tales of liberty will end in a plague of misery for us all." I'm not sure whether Bolivar actually said all this, or whether Gabriel Garcia Marquez put these words into Bolivar's mouth in his novel *The General in His Labyrinth*. Either way they ring true.

Ms. Fadiman's flag-raising is supported by such state-ments as George Parker's when he said that September 11th made it safe for Liberals to be patriotic. Is that the reason the Democrats barely raised their voices against the invasion of Iraq, a country that had nothing at all to do with 9/11, I wonder? I, as Noam Chomsky did, could never understand why I had to support my school's teams rather than admire the best team. I feel the same about countries. I have chosen Canada, which is not a bad choice, but other countries can do certain things better than we can, so why shouldn't I say so?

In her sensitive description of the family's flag-raising and her feelings as an ex-New Yorker about 9/11, not once did she mention what the motivation and feelings of the young men in the planes might have been. She is an educated woman. Is it rare for such a woman to consider all sides of the question, or is she like other "my country right or wrong" folk, just counting American bodies to the exclusion of Al Qaeda ones? Her history of the American flag is meticulous, but does she really understand the Liberal Supreme Court Justice, Anthony Kennedy, when he explains that burning the American flag is allowable since Americans believe in "law and peace and that freedom which sustains the human spirit"? Her upbringing, while Liberal, may not run to that much tolerance of dissent.

At the end of essay on the American flag, Ms. Fadiman checks the flag and finds it is a Dura-lite flag. I had hoped that the flag had been made in China, but it was not. It was made in the USA.

Although in my childhood I could recognize the flags of many countries, I find them disturbing symbols of nationhood. When it comes to the Stars and Stripes, and when it comes to my feelings towards America I lean somewhat towards Heather Mallick's, but still I can't quite explain the small lump that comes into my throat occasionally when I look at those two red bars and the red maple leaf in between, on my own flag.

I hate nationalism intensely, so what causes that lump? I suppose being born a Jew in a xenophobic country (England) already set my mind to seeing the damage the policy "my country right or wrong" had wrought in their far-flung empire. Later, as an immigrant to one of England's colonies, and far away from European nationalism, the clarity of the dangers of nationalism became even clearer. The European Union can only be a step in the right direction for solving problems by compromise rather than aggression.

If you really want to match Heather Mallick's vitriolitic attack on America, you might read Ronald Wright's blistering history, *What is America?: A Short History of the New World Order.* This history accentuates the division between the whites and the native peoples and imported slaves. Or you could read Howard Zinn's *A People's History of American Empire,* which plays the capitalists against the workers. Somewhere there must be a history of America where the whole of the people are not tarred as bigots and racists. I imagine a history which accentuates decent Americans – American humanitarians, creative Americans, Americans who achieved much in the way of scientific research, politicians who were not divisive. Well, the last is asking a bit much, I must admit. I will continue to search for such a book. If you know of one, please tell me immediately.

## ⊪⊿⊪\

Next, from my book-box, I pick up one of Steven Pinker's tomes, *The Stuff of Thought: Language as a Window into Human Nature.* Well actually I need both hands to do this for it is over four hundred pages. I settle in the corner of the couch and pull Eli's afghan over my legs. I am in for a long haul. When I get a large book, or a large project, come to that, I insulate myself from the world and create my own little safe haven. Of course, it never turns out to be safe for the project snarls or the book disturbs or, as in this case, disappoints. The first pages are brilliant, funny and entrancing, but by the time I have plodded through to page eighteen, I am sunk in a mesh of transitive and intransitive verbs and groupings that I will never remember and somehow his whole theory depends on me following him closely through the next three hundred and eighty-two pages. As it is unlikely I will be doing so, I close the book reluctantly, take myself off the couch and go upstairs and write a brilliant little poem about how I am not Margaret Atwood.

Eli comments wisely that even the most abstruse-subject book will have a beckoning first paragraph and that I had merely fallen for the promise once more.

## I'm not Margaret Atwood

"I'm not Margaret Atwood,"
I assure them earnestly,
meaning I am small of talent
and the same of fame.
I do, however, have curly hair
and am also a mother of a daughter.
Once, some years ago,
we, that is Margaret Atwood and I,
both applied for jobs at Bell Telephone.
Margaret was rejected being
overburdened with an MA.
I, with my simple BCom
was accepted, although my language,
they indicated, was a little odd.
And why not since I had
just disembarked from the immigrant ship,
*Samaria,* the week before and had
yet to add "Eh" to my verbal punctuation.
I didn't take the job,
but moved to Market Research,
where, apparently, Margaret too
found work and, at some other point,
we both back-to-the-landed,
although Margaret's domestic animals
far exceeded my pathetic brood of bantams.
I've probably written more books than she has,
although each had 1/10th of the pages
and 1/1000th of the sales... but still,
if Margaret Atwood had had
a very much smaller sister,
smaller in every way,
I might have been mistaken for her
by some provincial critic.

Today Sonja Arntzen, a professor of medieval Japanese literature, and I gave our double-header workshop on *tanka* and haiku. It was held upstairs in her waterfront log home. It is a simple home with a million-dollar view, filled with Japanese art. Upstairs the attendees gather around a wooden table beautifully built by a fellow-islander, Alan Brown. We are surrounded by stacks of ancient Japanese and Chinese texts, for Sonja's husband is also a professor, this time of Chinese medieval literature. What a couple. The attendees, we hope, will be inspired by the view. They don't disappoint, for they produce excellent tanka and haiku. Out of mutual respect, Sonja and I attend each other's workshop.

While we are on the subject of Japan, I have just come across a beautiful book, *The Art of the Gaman: Arts and Crafts from the Japanese American Internment Camps 1942-1946* by Delphine Hirasuna, Kit Hinrichs and Terry Heffernan, showing art done in the Japanese internment camps in the USA during World War II. One hundred and twenty thousand Japanese-Americans, two thirds of them US-born citizens, were interned. I have friends from the Canadian camps, and so look at the pictures of the carvings and paintings and basketry with care. Such creative forces overcoming the miseries of the camps are inspirational. The internment camps weren't Auschwitz, it's true, but they still represented a crazy side of humanity where fear takes over from reason, for there wasn't a single case ever reported of sabotage by the interned Japanese.

*Gaman* means "enduring the unbearable with patience and dignity" and one would need patience to carve hardwoods and stone to make jewellery and teapots, to cover wire with twisted crepe paper in order to make intricate baskets, to sew reeds with string from unravelled onion sacks, make knives from discarded animal traps ... patience to transmute an insult into works of art. In the internment camps, ordinary people became teachers for the others. One seventy-six-year-old man counted that he had had six hundred and fifty needlework students. Typing students, lacking typewriters, practised using key-circles drawn on scrap paper.

With sometimes ten thousand internees to the square mile, boredom threatened to convert to anger. Authorities allowed art schools to open and a full curriculum was offered from figure-drawing to fashion design. All of this happened within an atmosphere that could have tipped into despair. *The Art of Gaman* tells of these efforts. Read it and have some shame for your governments who used fear to terrorize an immigrant group.

It left me wondering why one doesn't hear of similar efforts in the camps the Palestinians occupy. Surely that trust in the healing power of creativity must exist amongst them also.

### ∭⊿∥∖

From time to time folks present me with books that have "saved their lives." Curious, I might read one, and then close the book gently and wonder what kind of life they must have been living in order to be saved by this book. Even if it is a bestseller, a Giller or Booker Prize winner, if it doesn't work for me, it is a real effort to discover why it works for others. By the way, if you need more spare time in life, stop feeling you have to read those prize-winning books or the *New York Times'* "Best Sellers" list or the most current hot book-of-the-day. You will be amazed how this frees your life up. A small volume that catches the eye, printed in say 1963, and written by a long-forgotten author, may be just the book that sends you spinning and turns your life upside down. By locking yourself into the *New York Time's* Best Sellers (perhaps influenced by the need to be *au courant*) or into The Classics (influenced by the need to be considered cultured) you are missing out on a whole slew of other wonderful writers. Learning to seek out the books that you want or need to read is a bit like finding your own voice. The reader is the final participant in the creation of a book and, as an aware reader, conscious of what you are bringing to the reading and what you expect from the book, you are playing an essential role in the whole process. Choose with care.

**ℿⅬ◢Ⅰ\**

When it comes to guilty feelings, I'm still feeling a little guilty about my rejection of *Dr. Faustus.* Guilt is not a good feeling to have lingering around, so I decide to commit myself to the new venture of reading the recent translation by Royall Tyler of *The Tale of Genji.* It is one thousand and two hundred pages long, so I feel this is a reasonable substitution for *Dr. Faustus.* I know I stand a chance of completing the book because I have read it several times before in other translations. It is one of the most important classics in Japanese literature, and arguably the world's first novel.

ⅡↀⅡↀ

De Bernières' *Captain Corelli's Mandolin* still lingers in my mind, so I get the DVD that had been made from it. It disappointed. I spoke about this with my son, who is a movie enthusiast. He advised me to "always see the movie first. The number of books that have been successfully adapted to screen I can count on one hand." As eighty-five percent of movies are adaptations of books, or comics, I thought this was probably good advice. It was only after I had rung off that I realised the predicament my son had left me in. It meant I could not see a movie of any of the thousands of books I have read in my lifetime without experiencing some degree of disappointment. I decided that a little disappointment was acceptable and started counting for myself the successful movie adaptations of stories that I had already read: *Pride and Prejudice, One Flew Over the Cuckoo's Nest, Brokeback Mountain, To Kill a Mocking Bird, Remains of the Day, Schindler's List* (based on *Schindler's Ark*) … well one shouldn't always take one's children's advice literally, for see I am now already on to my second set of fingers. *The Manchester Guardian* has made a list of the fifty best film adaptations. I am pleased to see that it contains some of my choices.

I have just remembered that Graham Greene's *The Third Man* went the other way, being a movie before it was a book and the same with Arthur C. Clarke's *2001: A Space Odyssey.* Both Greene and Clarke wrote the movie scripts themselves. I haven't read the books, but note in my notebook to do so when I have a free moment, in order to decide whether they were better than the movies.

It does feel, however, as Charlie Jane Anders says, that "the movie industry is a huge maw – sucking up every stray thought or tingle of creativity that anyone has ever had, and mashing them all into new reasons for Brad Pitt to grimace."

Apparently, movies of around one hundred minutes need only one hundred pages of text. Adaptations don't, however, just eliminate scenes from the book, they also add them for sex interest, say, or because a leading actor is taking a minor role and demands more screen time. The film may also introduce an entirely new character to perhaps act as a kind of Greek chorus. If the book is more monologue than action, much is lost in the move from book to film unless thoughts are indicated by a narrator, or voice-over. Other reasons for books being unsuccessful when adapted for film are that they may be too full of ideas, that they are just not visual enough, or are too far away from the mainstream. I am thinking of books like Olaf Stapledon's *Starmaker,* a cult book in its time, and very influential with subsequent science-fiction writers. I don't think anyone has ever attempted to make a movie of it. It was just too abstract.

Paul Schrader's rule for adapting a book to a movie is that "a film scene should be like a party. You arrive late and leave early! That helps to get to the crux fast and know what to lose." Some folks even recommend that the director ignore the book totally and just take the rough story over to the medium he/she knows best. Of course, the better known the book, the more the audience will demand an exact adaptation. I myself feel that even if the adaptation has strayed from the theme, or message of the book, at least the story's "soul" should have come through. I can't define this, but the hairs on my arms usually indicate when it has happened.

# February

February, even on the balmy west coast of Canada, can bring on the blues and demands cheerful reading, perhaps picking up on the never-ending love expectations of Valentine's Day. For this reason, I turn to one of my favourite love stories. Well, actually, love is but a small part of John le Carré's *The Little Drummer Girl,* which I am reading probably for the fourth or fifth time. Why do I love it so much? It isn't just that it presents a balanced picture of the Palestine/Israeli situation, for my general feeling is a pox on both sides for not settling things reasonably. Nor is it that it is a page-turning story with a wonderfully tensioned romance (though it is both). I think what draws me to it is the role-playing. The characters change identity several times during the story, so that one is left wondering which one is the real personality in each case. My husband is a linear man at all times, so when I insisted (a thing I rarely do with him) that he read *The Little Drummer Girl,* he was compelled to get little cards on which he listed the characters as they came up, and their name changes as they developed, in order to keep tabs on them. He reads lying down on his stomach on the bed, with the book on the floor at the head of the bed (along with the cards) and it was amusing to watch him shuffle the cards and make copious notes as he turned the pages. Since my husband lay reading this way as a child, a way that necessitates the bed being away from the wall, I have given up having a headboard for our bed and so being able to read in bed myself, in order to preserve my second marriage.

## ALAN

Thinking of John le Carré's spies and Cold War tales reminded me that when I was five years old, I went from door to door in our neighbourhood, with my half-sisters, collecting donations for the Spanish Civil War. I was allowed to carry the tin can with its slit in the top for coins. I was bemused about what the money was to be used for and, indeed, was bemused about what the war was all about. Ever since that time, I have been oddly resistant to finding answers to those very questions. Over the years I have learned bits and pieces about that period – the waste of young men in futile battle, that Hitler tested his latest weaponry in Spain in order to be ready for his all-out assault on Europe a couple of years later, and I heard of General Francisco Franco's brutality. But I have resisted acquiring more exact details, perhaps not wanting to know what a waste of time my little tin-can effort was. But today I am going on an adventure to break through that block and really find out for myself what happened in Spain in the thirties, for I have acquired a large book enti-tled *The Spanish Civil War* by Hugh Thomas. I do hope these five hundred pages will finally enlighten me.

This book seems to have come from the library of the London School of Economics. How did it land up on this little island of Gabriola? I had aspired to go to that very left-wing school of learning. But that was in the late '40s, when soldiers returning to civilian life were being given priority at universities. Places at the London School of Economics filled quickly, and so I, a civilian schoolgirl, had to be content with Birmingham University, my second choice, which was founded for the education of workers' children.

ⅢⅡⅢ

My island contains a remarkable bunch of people. Among them are the retired professor of medieval Japanese literature and the retired professor of Chinese literature I mentioned earlier. I had come across an essay by Ou-yang Hsiu and, admiring this writer's style, asked Professor Lynn if he had any more works by this man. He, of course, had, and so I am ploughing through a learned dissertation, *The Literary Works of Ou-yang Hsiu (1007-72)* by Ronald C. Egan, which tells me a little more than I had asked to know about the man. Being told a little more than one needs to know about a subject can be irritating, but it's usually not a bad thing. Occasionally I feel a little faint, or even a little nauseated while reading, and it is often because I am being fed more than I can take in. It also might indicate that I am getting out of my depths. Sometimes I pull back, but if I proceed, I usually come out with some gem of wisdom and a feeling of minor triumph that I didn't give up my struggle with the text.

Ou-yang Hsiu was a renaissance man. Not only did he rise to high office despite being almost self-taught, but he was also an historian and was considered a master of prose and poetry. I think it is his poetry I am most attracted to, for it is humorous and self-deprecatory and resonates with me. It was an essay, however, that had first drawn me to Ou-yang. I enjoy the way his essays seem to have no strategy and just wander disconnectedly, often starting with a topic far from his intended subject. By the end, however, he has drawn it all together and his intent is clear.

In *The Literary Works,* I came across this quote that sent me off at a tangent, "Man-ch'ing used wine to conceal himself from the world, and Pi-yen used Buddhism." I use frankness and fast talk. Susan Musgrave says she conceals her vulnerability with vulnerability. Another comment on Ou-yang that reverberated with me was that he edited his pieces so many times that "in some cases, by the time he was finished, not a single one of the original words remained."

On speaking of poetry, Ou-yang Hsiu says it "pricks the eyes and lances the heart." Would I could write poetry like that. But, of course, I shouldn't feel like that, for Ou-yang, speaking of another man, says, "He was a man just as I am. If he was capable of it, how should I be incapable?" That's what I tell my students in my writing classes, and then I go home and tell myself.

**∥◁∥**

I had just written to David Cobb, an English haiku writer, to ask permission to use one of his brilliant haiku in a new manuscript I was preparing. We decided to exchange recent books, as poets are wont to do. His, *Business in Eden,* arrived and I eagerly devoured it. I am given to gobbling down such books and then masticating them slowly with my second-reading-stomach somewhat later. His book was in the form of *haibun* – diary-like essays punctuated with haiku.

I was overwhelmed with the intensity of these haibun. Even though I am familiar with the form, I had never read anything quite like this before. It was as if some of the very soil of East Anglia (I'll slip Essex, perhaps wrongly, in here), where David lives, had risen, put on bicycle clips and taken itself for a small cycling trip over its own familiar land, so deeply rooted is David in his environment and history. I was so drawn into his writing that I went to the trouble of digging out a map of the UK, so I could follow the ancient trails that he had taken.

When, in the first haibun, "Spring Journey to the Saxon Shore," I came to the line in David's prose from George Borrow's *Lavengro: The Scholar, the Gypsy, the Priest,* "Life is very sweet, brother," I let loose a flood of tears and the previous lines to the quote, "There's night and day, brother, both sweet things; sun, moon and stars, brother, all sweet things; there's likewise a wind on the heath," wandered through my collapsed mind. I know all this sounds very dramatic, but, for a moment, I was engulfed by the realisation that although I myself was born in Essex, at Walthamstow, and lived some years at Thorpe Bay, and though the first twenty-two years of my life were spent being educated in the UK, there is not one cell of my body that is English. This is because my grandparents came seeking a haven from the European pogroms as immigrants in the 1890s and my parents settled uneasily into attempted assimilation (an impossibility with England's xenophobia and strong class structure). David could trace his family back to the sixteenth century, I could trace mine back to the 1890s and then only because my grandfather got tricked into buying tickets to England, when he thought he was bound for America.

Years later I reached the Americas and lemming-like finished up on the west coast. I was not tempted to jump, because I had lived in Japan and knew I was more than ever a *gaijin* (outsider) there. Oh David, how I envy you your solid roots that give firm ground to your wit and compassion. Shadows and contours are filled with ancestors for you, whereas for me they are a blur of possible shtetls in that boundary land where wonder-rabbis held court.

> shadow-lined ditches
> the indelible contours
> of our ancestors
>
> *David Cobb*

Even today I have only First Nation clamming grounds to offer on my chosen island home compared with David's churches, castles and ancient cottages. Another root holding David firmly in place is his faith, or at least his custom of churchgoing, which provides a slightly firmer base than my floating agnosticism.

David, like I am, is deeply immersed in the haiku world and glimpses of Matsuo Bashō and Kobayashi Issa peek through his writing. For example, the man pointing the way with the nail in the haibun, "Away to go," reflects Issa's radish-picker pointing the way with a radish. David's very first haiku in this book, in fact, reflects Bashō's very first haiku, both being about dolls.

David's lines:

**all that now remains
of a warrior's wrath**

remind me strongly of Bashō's haiku:

**summer grasses
dream traces
of ancient warriors**

*(translated by Sonja Arntzen
and Naomi Beth Wakan)*

I was glad David mentioned Bashō's pomposity when speaking of his poem about prostitutes. I've always found Bashō very conscious of his own dignity, much more so than Issa and Yosa Buson, who are more natural.

David's firm grounding in Saxon earth, coupled with his experience with a foreign form of poetry, haiku from Japan, allows his writing to offer a sense of familiarity, while at the same time, layering it with a shadow of the exotic.

David's haibun are concentrated with literary references, in fact he so often speaks directly to writers throughout this book (such as the poet Edward Benlowes), that it is no wonder that the footnotes are copious. "A Day in Twilight," the second lengthy haibun in *Business in Eden,* is dense with beings once real or once imagined.

His prose is as poetic as his haiku. Take for example, the line "wake of drake cross-hatching wake of duck." There's a haiku tucked away in there, and there also is in his phrase, "the pewtery chinking of some wren" if I knew what "chinking" was. Have I left so much of England behind that I have no idea what many of his words mean? What, for example, is a "spicing cup" and what a "withdrawing cake"? Google couldn't even help with them. And what is the meaning of "clunch" and "bangling over the ankles"? I suspect that David probably invented these onomatopoeic words.

As to the author's wit and compassion, his haibun on family carols is heartbreaking, as he almost carries his aged mother to the service. His wit sparkles throughout the book, but particularly in his haibun on "The School Christmas Show." Children's errors are easy targets for humour, we know, but in this piece David excels himself.

nativity play
red face of the angel
   coming on too soon

Towards the end, David speaks of Shelley's idea that poets of all ages contribute to one Great Poem perpetually in progress. That does slot us all in together rather nicely. However it is with the shadows (shadows of the past, shadows of himself) that David is most at home, I suspect:

the shortest day
almost no time at all
to have a shadow

*David Cobb*

I always wanted to write a "tour de force" but never have. David's book of haibun, *Business in Eden,* can only be so described.

## ∏⊿∏\

Staying with English writers for a while, I have just completed Ann Thwaite's biography of A. A. Milne. He and I have several things in common; things such as our child-like naivety and having *Pride and Prejudice* as one of our all-time favourite books. Milne was described by W. A. Darlington as "always an autobiographical writer." Perhaps that is why I like him so much, because I also favour that form of writing.

Milne was also accused of being drugged on nostalgia, which is where we part ways, for I always seem to be living six months ahead, partly on hope and partly because I have to plan future readings that have been booked for me to give. His nostalgia, I think, came from the horrors he experienced during the First World War, which subsequently left him with a yearning for the mythical time of a perfect childhood, with nannies and nursery teas and things such as those that pervade his children's books.

Milne's writing for children affected my generation strongly. Even in my secular household, a framed copy of

"Vespers" hung between my bed and my twin's. By the time I had reached university, Christopher Robin had been almost canonized. I distinctly remember the Pooh books being used as text in a series of child psychology lectures that I attended.

Back to Thwaite, I loved A. A. M.'s quote in her book, "a mile from fame and an inch from obscurity" – aren't most poets in that position? I find that Milne also had a lot of my Puritanism and shyness. His reluctance to listen to grubby jokes and his inability to share the joys of bars and brothels with his fellow soldiers was well expressed when he said, "When I am told, as I so often am, that it is time that I 'came to grips' with real life – preferably in a brothel, or a public bar, where life is notoriously more real than elsewhere, minds more complex, more imaginative, more articulate, soul nearer the stars – I realized sadly that, I should bring back nothing but the same self to which objection had already been taken." I love this quote as I have always wondered what "growing up" really meant when I view corrupt politicians and spin-advertising protecting crummy products and ... the list is endless.

Of course Ann Thwaite's book is full of A. A. Milne quotes, many of which appeal to me both from my experience with writing and the writer's world, and with my understanding of his yearning for an Eden of a childhood; a time when all was in its right place. For example, on authors, he comments, "No sensible author wants anything but praise." Yes, few ask for criticism, and fewer still, if they get it, take it and do something with it. About voice, Milne states, "However long a writer has been in business, he is still without authority for anybody but himself. All he knows is how to write in his own way." He adds, "However proud he may be of earlier work, it is praise of his latest book that he appreciates most." The doubt whether their new book will equal if not exceed the last in excellence, the doubt whether a next book will, indeed, ever be completed are the doubts of every writer.

Lest you think recalling A. A. Milne, as I have done, is a personal quirky thing to do, then you perhaps haven't read the furious comments on the recent sequel to *The House at Pooh Corner,* which have almost exceeded protests about the G8. The book is called *Return to the Hundred Acre Wood,* and is by David Benedictus. According to Maria Nikolajeva, who has taught Milne's work for thirty years and is currently a professor of education at Cambridge University, "It's absolutely the best book ever written, and I mean it ... All the primary things that are necessary for human life are there ... It's a philosophical book, it's a book with incredible depth, and it's a pity if it's misinterpreted as light entertainment."

You may not like the idea of a sequel to *The House at Pooh Corner,* but the trustees of Pooh property have long wanted one, and decreed that it might go ahead. The last Pooh book was published in 1928 and this new book came out in 2009. Such long-lasting popularity of a character is explained by the fact that Winnie-the-Pooh has become an intrinsic part of culture, or at least of British culture. I'm not sure how all this is controlled or affected by Disney's dismal handling of the characters, but I promise myself to look into it sometime.

## ɪ⊿ɪ

For those of you vaguely interested, I have to report that I am up to page two hundred and fifty in my reading of *The Tale of Genji*. This book was written by Murasaki Shikibu, a Heian court woman. The irony is that at that time, women were not encouraged to learn the Chinese script of men and scholars, in fact a "women's hand" was invented for their lesser abilities. In spite of this condescension, those Heian court women produced some wonderful books and outshone the male writers at that time, even though men had the skill of using *kanji*.

## ɪ⊿ɪ

We go into the village on Gabriola once a week, on Saturdays, for shopping, Post Office, bank business, library exchange and gossip. Last week while I was waiting in the library for Eli, I glanced over its modest magazine rack and thought how it represented the folk on Gabriola so well. Gulf Islands are small worlds to themselves, each with its own peculiar characteristics, and I do mean peculiar.

Our small library is wedged between the local liquor store and the hardware store in our folklife village. This is a set of shops and a wooden boardwalk that was imported, plank-by-plank from the 1986 Expo site in Vancouver. Reassembled it looks like a small-town centre in a western movie. At Expo it was where the folksingers hung out.

Back to the magazine rack. It obviously mirrors the more literate islanders. We have the usual back-to-the-land magazines reflecting all the earnest city intellectuals trying to survive on their large pensions and small plots of vegetables. Then we have magazines for the soul – *Resurgence* and such 'spiritual' magazines, although I was aghast to find this magazine didn't pay its contributors (when I had had an article accepted by it) even though it carried pages of ads. I suppose there are 'spiritual situations' and then there are 'spiritual situations!'

Since there are many artists settled on our island, there are the arts and crafts magazines – *Threads, Fibrearts, Canadian Art* and similar journals. Gulf Islanders often find themselves on islands because they are protesting folks in power, whether it be political power or cliques in their particular professions. For those, I notice *Utne Reader* and *Adbusters.* As the library has a limited budget, a pile of donated *Economists, Time* magazines and *Macleans* reflect our more conventional citizens, but what are we to make of an enormous set of *Architectural Digest?* I'm sure we have a few millionaires on the island, mostly Albertans and Americans fresh from the oil fields and mines (that is the owning of shares in, rather than the grubby working in), but mostly those folks fly in by seaplane and stay sequestered in their waterfront properties. Still houses on our island tend to lean (quite literally) towards the self-built, or built-in-stages as the kids come or go or the income flushes out with some small inheritance. For these folk who have built, or are building, their own home, the library hopefully supplies *Fine Homebuilding* and for the furniture to go inside, *Fine Woodworking*. I mustn't forget those islanders who build their own boats, for there sits *WoodenBoat* magazine ready for them. Gabriola has the only wooden boat-building school in Canada, as well as a log-house-building school.

On the island, almost everyone who is not madly in love with deer has a fence and, at least, a flower garden. Our Garden Club is the largest single-interest group and its members, I am happy to report, are wholesome, friendly, knowledgeable and decent. For them the library carries *GardenWise, Garden West* and, for those who are into live-stock and veggies, *Harrowsmith Country Life* and *Mother Earth News*.

Children are cherished and encouraged here, and there are many families that home-school and who, of course, have asked that *Home Education Magazine* be present on the magazine racks. Our island children, being superior, also have *Owl* and *YES* magazines sitting available for them, or at least for their keen parents. The library also carries *TransWorld Skateboarding* for a range of ages, as Gabriola, though it may be lacking in other respects, has its own skateboard site.

My own choices? Well *Scientific American* sits there for my own, and my husband's edification, and as a nice balance to our artistic endeavours. I never take out *Writer's Digest* as the more hopeful of the up-and-coming island writers do, for I know that magazine and all its offspring, such as *Writer's Yearbook*, are mainly in the business of making money for themselves. The articles rarely even interest, let alone encourage me to stick at the machine, as

I do, everyday. I don't subscribe to magazines myself, so while waiting in the library for my husband to finish gossiping (men do seem to hang around chewing the cud even more than women here) I'm drawn to *Fibrearts* and *Canadian House & Home,* and, as I said, occasionally I'll pick up *Scientific American,* which has become much more approachable in recent years.

So yes, our island is well-provided by its magazine shelves at the library, but mostly it is favoured by its wonderful librarian and library assistants who, by some remarkable feat of memory, are able to greet everyone by name as they enter the door, and have suggestions galore for each person's reading predilections. That's what makes our little island library so irresistible on our Saturday jaunts into the village for supplies and gossip.

# March

I'm fretting to get going in the garden – fiddling with seed packages, and longing for frost-free nights. To stabilize my erratic behaviour, I settle down to Czerny studies on the piano and, as accompaniment, have turned to a book on music, Alex Ross' *The Rest is Noise: Listening to the Twentieth Century,* a history of music in the twentieth century. I am astonished to read of the amount of political-ization of music that has occurred. I am familiar with the art and writing world and the fact that some folk will do anything (including modifying their creative style) in order to get a commission or contract, or merely an invitation to an "in" gathering, so I wonder why I am so naive about the music world. I certainly knew about music under the Nazis (as Jews, Wagner was never played in our musical home), but not so familiar with music in the Stalin era. I was, however, deeply immersed in the abstract art period, and God forbid you painted still life during that time, so I shouldn't be so amazed at the viciousness of say, Pierre Boulez towards composers who wrote tonally, unlike his own atonal music.

The book clearly indicates that the line between folk, classical and pop music is blurred these days and perhaps there are so many styles of music being written now that it really is a free-for-all and so one doesn't have to sell one's own style out in order to "get on." I can only commiserate with all the lost talent that got shut out of the scene because it wasn't of the prevailing school of composing.

In a parallel to music, the edges of writing genres also seem to be blurring a little, with page and performance poets now drawing closer, fiction appearing based on fact, and poetry sometimes approaching essays, while essays close in on poetry. As far as poetry goes, while I have trouble with academic poetry which is often too abstruse for me, and I have a certain distaste for rhymed poetry, I would never deny that these kinds of poetry were poetry and had a validity of their own. There is room within creativity for the many forms it takes. A dominant clique should not be able to determine what is acceptable and what is not. I sigh, knowing that "fashion" is the everyday word for this and that cycles of the "acceptable" seem inevitable whether it be in atonal music or skirt lengths.

In *The Rest is Noise,* I come across Alex Ross' quote, "The proximity of terror does not obligate the artist to make terror his subject," and am glad that I write about robins and eagles and clothespin bags in a world that still uses violence as a way of dealing with greed. As if greed can ever be dealt with, for it seems to be a basic evolutionary factor.

The musing on tolerance of other styles of creativity, particularly in one's own field, has me winging off, wondering why fiction stays an elusive genre for me. These thoughts bring me a flash image of twins, that is me and my own twin. My twin was an extension of myself and vice versa and so we had to split for many years in order to complete ourselves as individual personalities. Even when that was vaguely accomplished, we still both have the tendency to treat everyone in our own lives as extensions of ourselves. This leads to us having firm expectations of others (as they are merely parts of ourselves, rather like the Canadarm is to the space station) and when those expectations are not met, we feel more confused and rejected than would be normal for the situation. It seems that everyone is a figment of our imagination, or at least a character that should fit into our plot. Since everyone is fictitious, myself included (since I am my own fiction), what need is there to write fiction? And that is my present insight into my inability to write fiction, and I am sticking to it.

## ∏∐∆∥∖

Back to the topic of politics in art, I am wondering whether when I write a haiku such as:

power outage
on the solar radio
Eine Kleine Nachtmusik

I would be thought of as making a political statement about the inadequacy of BC Hydro and the BC government when it comes to keeping the power lines on our island free of the swaying branches. Under Stalin, would such a witty haiku have sent me to a gulag?

By the way, a description of what might be called personal politics in the arts (which is really what Pierre

Boulez's blackballing of the tonalists was all about) can be read about in *The Anthologist,* the brilliant little exposition promoting rhymed poetry, which appears in the guise of a novel. In this book, Nicholson Baker speaks of "the Pound-Eliot-Joyce axis" as if "getting-on" in the poetry world is indeed warfare.

Another matter completely, but I love John Cage's quote that is mentioned in *The Rest is Noise,* "Wherever we are, what we hear is mostly noise. When we ignore it, it disturbs us. When we listen to it, we find it fascinating."

## ꟼL⊿I⟊

Why do librarians stick their bar code over the book's title? Obviously because it makes it easier for them to check books out that way. But for us, the clients, it means we take home a box of books with titles such as: *The Eq[bar code] that couldn't be solved,* and *The Book of [bar code]* and unfortunate authors whose names are Nichola [bar code] and Armand Mari[bar code].

I love the librarians who work at our little library dearly and know that it is not they who plaster the bar code with such gay abandon on the top right-hand corner of every book, but still.

## ꟼL⊿I⟊

A hiatus while I take a working holiday, including a presentation on writing as an older person, at a book festival. I tell how an inadvertently forwarded email describes me as "a lovely old biddy from Gabriola" to much laughter from my audience. I also launch my new book, *Compositions: Notes on the written word*. There are three other "noted" authors also presenting, along with a bunch of teens who are included in a teen anthology of angst-ridden poetry. Did I really feel like that when I was a teen? Doting parents are not what I need for my book launch; however I warm them up with my poem "Sex after 70," and do make some sales.

One of the two highlights at the book festival for me was the meeting with Robert Priest, an Ontario poet of wit and protest, who read a poem in which the New Testament is told backwards (starting with the resurrection and finishing with Jesus in the womb) and he followed this with an anti-Lord's Prayer – irreverent and very funny. The other highlight of the festival for me was lighting upon the book *From Man to Man,* written by Moishe Nadir. I have never heard of this author, but his prose poems blow me away and I swear I will never write the same way again after picking up this book. Where has he been all my life? Apparently tucked away in the Yiddish writers' ghetto in New York. This is surely not his first book that has been translated? I check, and apparently it is. I eagerly await the second. What is the lazy translator doing? I need that second book as a thirsty person needs ... well Nadir would never use such a cliché.

On returning home I write to the guy who translated the book, urging him onwards and also to the guy who helped edit *From Man to Man.* I pour out my situation of being in a position where I am neither completely accepted by the Jewish, nor the non-Jewish worlds. I have never poured out angst to a stranger before, and will not do it again, for the editor, not hearing where I am at (maybe he didn't read my email fully), replies by inviting me to a Purim party in Victoria.

How rarely do we find a person who really "hears" us when we need to be heard. Later I send a review of a book to a magazine editor. It is an odd review, but he really hears what I want to say and so, taking a risk, accepts it.

A last word on Nadir and his wonderful prose poems. My favorite is number XXXIII where he describes how Life gets dressed up and goes to the theatre, where apparently he sees and hears of things that he had never experienced before. At the end of the performance, Life can only conclude that he has no idea how to live and would have to go to the theatre more often to see how it is done. Nadir concludes with the caustic comment, "and from day to day Life became more interesting ◊ more sophisticated ◊ more theatrical." Nadir apparently used ◊ as his favourite punctuation mark.

Later, I am still so enamoured with Moishe Nadir that I read a whole prose poem of his to a couple of Japanese academics who are visiting our studio, much to their bemusement. I read it with such feeling that I felt they must be able to see just how imaginative and creative a writer Nadir is. They looked stunned, but after my powerful reading, the man merely asks me, "Naomi-san, when did you first become interested in things Japanese?" I looked at him with equal astonishment.

I have been reading a book entitled *1001 Books You Must Read Before You Die* (general editor – Peter Boxall) and, of course, it filled me with guilt and remorse. What have I been doing with my life that I have probably not read more than one third of the books included? Guilt is not a good thing to feel, so, thinking I shouldn't waste time actually counting how many books that I might have read at least halfway through from the one thousand and one presented, I settled down and decided that the least thing I could do was to read the 1001 three-hundred-word critiques of the novels – these alone stretch to nine hundred and sixty pages, and that, I thought, would be enough to at least have paid token homage to the novel as it has developed over the era of *Homo sapiens.*

Before I settled on to my reading couch and reached for the afghan that I had knitted for my husband which he rarely uses, I did muse that had I started reading these one thousand and one novels by the time I was, say, seven years old (by which time I was already perusing George Bernard Shaw and the other Fabians that my left-wing-bending half-sisters had pressed into my precocious little hands), and had I read one of these one thousand and one novels every twenty-eight days of my life, I would have read them all by now and would therefore be able to die in peace. But what kind of life would have been devoted entirely to reading one thousand and one novels? No husbands, no divorces, no mortgage, why it would have been a wretched existence.

By the time, a week later, that I had read the summaries of the one thousand and one novels, a few odd ideas had popped into my busy little mind. The first idea was that somewhere, on some hidden shelf of our house, in some box in the corner of the basement, I had the manuscript for a novel that I had actually written myself. This idea must have arisen because I had allowed the one thousand and one plots (some of them somewhat similar, for after all there are only so many ways humans can humiliate or empower each other) to swirl around my brain until I had half-imagined the plot of a novel I had possibly written myself. It was about a man and a woman and an adopted child and a missing twin and a small-state revolution in which the man and the woman lose the adopted child and find the missing twin – well it developed somewhat along those lines. I know, in reality, I have not written this novel, for I only write essays and poetry, but still that's what reading the summary of one thousand and one famous novels can do to you.

At one reading I was giving, a small precocious child told me that he wrote fiction, and asked whether I did. I said that I did not. He then pressed me by asking why I had not been able to write fiction and, as I was not about to be upstaged by any bright ten year old, I told him that my whole life was a fiction and therefore I did not need to write fiction. I had not the slightest idea what I meant, but I was mean enough to smile slightly when I saw a bemused frown come onto his earnest young face.

The other thought that occurred to me after I had read the summaries of *1001 Books You Must Read Before You Die* was the tragedy of all the other novelists who had not had their books included; all the medium important novelists that merely filled publishers' lists so that the publisher could concentrate on their bestsellers. And not just all the medium-level novelists, how about all the writers who had devoted their creative energies to writing for children? Very few of these had been listed.

My mind does not work linearly, and so I was not surprised to find myself thinking of a neighbour. This neighbour turns up at weddings and birthdays and funerals on our little island, with an appropriate, and often witty, piece of doggerel. Once I advised her to gather these pieces together, but she scoffed at the idea, disclaiming that they were any good, and telling me that she'd only done half a dozen anyway. Some months after I had given her my advice, she rang in great excitement, for she had gathered the doggerel together and actually had fifty, and her husband was preparing them for a small book. So we discussed how to produce a chapbook and I distinctly heard the sounds of a writer being born. Her chapbook, however, would never have been included in *The 1001 Books You Must Read Before You Die.* So, I then paused a moment in order to tip my hat in homage to all the wonderful unsung amateur writers not included in the book.

Reading this book, *The 1001 Books You Must Read Before You Die,* that had produced so much guilt in me, left me with the feeling that I would like to have written a novel. That is true of most of the people who come to my writing workshops; they all would love to have written a novel, but I, and they, hadn't had the discipline, the rigor, the masochism to sit at a desk for a year, or two, and write at least one page a day. One page a day and even after vigorous editing, you would have a novel, or at least a novella, written. Think of that! I did. And picking phrases at random from *1001 Books You Must Read Before You Die,* I imagined that I had written a novel that "blasted open 'official truths' with the force of a carnival out of control." Sophie Thomas said this of Mikhail Bulgakov's *The Master and Margarita* as her contribution to the one thousand and one books. Or perhaps someone would say that I had "commented acerbically on colonialism." Yes, that would be nice. Or perhaps I had even written a novella so that Garth Twa could have said about me, as he said about Zadie Smith, "The maturity and scope of her talent seems preternatural."

But that is not to be, for here I am, yet once more, turning out yet one more little essay about books and writers and, do you know, having recovered from reading the summaries of one thousand and one books by triumphant (and often alcoholic and suicidal) authors, I am quite content to have my life running this way.

## ⁄ILⴰⵏ\

Pursuing my interest in the Milnes, I have just finished the last of Christopher Robin Milne's three books. This one, *The Enchanted Places* (the other two are *The Path Through the Trees* and *Hollow on the Hill: The Search for a Personal Philosophy*), covers the years with his parents, his willingness to go along with being Christopher Robin at first and then his years of disenchantment so that he never saw his mother again after his father's funeral. She lived, I believe, another fifteen years. Although he had, as a young child, enjoyed the fame that his father's books had brought to him, after his wartime experiences in World War II, he grew to hate his father and considered that he had been grossly exploited as a child.

All his own books have the same childlikeness of his father's famous four volumes and Christopher Robin Milne stayed a "pure," "innocent" and "principled" man all his life. His early thrust into the world's limelight resulted in a later quiet withdrawal into a small bookstore in a rural town.

Milne's *Path Through the Trees* is about his adult life and in it he doesn't spend much time complaining about his father's exploitations and his mother's distance. His third book, *Hollow on the Hill,* concerns his personal philosophy. Apparently he has a fourth book, *The Windfall: A Fable* (his own favourite), which I hadn't heard about. It is a reinterpretation of the Adam and Eve story. I make a note to order it, liking a certain completion in my reading habits.

I was left wondering about the relationship between fathers and sons who were both writers, thinking of Kingsley and Martin Amis (Kingsley pronounced his son's books unreadable) and Evelyn and Auberon Waugh and grandson Alexander (who actually wrote about his literary forebears in *Fathers and Sons: The Autobiography of a Family*). A. A. Milne and Christopher Robin Milne don't seem to quite fit in here since their writings didn't overlap. Perhaps Christopher had to wait a while to let resentment cool down before he started to tell of his own life.

## ⚏

Whenever I'm despondent about the world, I pick up my copy of *Dragonhunt* by Frances (Sandy) Duncan, of our very own little island. She herself has probably long ago forgotten the book that she wrote, although it must have served the same purpose for her at one time that it does for me every time I read it, which is the healing together of my scattered bits. Individuation, Jung might have called it, and *Dragonhunt* does the job every time. It is the tale of two dysfunctional people who come together for a moment of true blending which thrusts them apart, each into their own completions. Well, that's my take on it, and because that is how I interpret it, that is how the book works for me.

The surrealistic characters placed in the familiar setting of the Canadian west coast don't bother me. I take them literally, can see them clearly and when they dissolve into their own beings, I am left with myself in a quiet place, where all possibilities seem very probable.

## ⚏

As I replace *Dragonhunt* on my bookshelf, I see that a copy of *For Whom the Bell Tolls* is next to it. This starts me re-evaluating Hemingway, whom I consider second-rate compared to Somerset Maugham, who is usually given that stamp. My Maugham section far exceeds my Hemingways. I have taken a second look at *For Whom the Bell Tolls, The*

*Sun Also Rises* and others and find Maugham's *The Painted Veil, Moon and Sixpence,* etc., much more satisfying. Maugham's less macho heroes tend to stand up better over the years and Hemingway's straying female characters just seem pointless in a world that was soon to experience Auschwitz and Stalin's gulags. Maugham may have been sardonic and a bit of a misanthrope, but his characters, particularly his women, are better fleshed out than Hemingway's and his much deeper understanding of humanity compares favourably with Hemingway's heavy-handedness.

ⵏⵍⵣⵉⵏ

For those of you following my progress, I have to report that I am now halfway through *The Tale of Genji.* One can only read it in brief portions, since characters are usually indicated by position rather than name. This necessitates flipping back to the beginning of each chapter to remind oneself who the Minister of the Right or the Lady of the Sixth Ward really are (a list of characters that will appear in each chapter is given at the beginning of the chapter), and this gets to be a little tiresome. The translation is brilliant, however, and brings the Heian Court to life far better that any of the other translations I have read.

ⵏⵍⵣⵉⵏ

I seem to have too much time on my hands, for I find myself making a list of writers who were destroyed by alcohol or drugs, and look on it with wonder. Is it that, as Steven Levy put it, "creativity is pain"? No, that can't be so, because many writers managed to stay creative without substance abuse, writers such as Mark Twain, Saul Bellow and James Michener. On the other side we have Hemingway (who portrayed some of his characters, such as Jake Barnes and Brett Ashley, as alcoholics) and F. Scott Fitzgerald, Dylan Thomas and Truman Capote, Dorothy Parker and James Joyce, Jack Kerouac, Raymond Chandler, Tennessee Williams ... the list seems endless. Donald W. Goodwin declared that alcoholism was an epidemic among twentieth-century writers. I wonder whether this is still true as we move into the twenty-first-century, or whether drug addiction has overtaken alcoholism. Bartenders seem to be the only people that can out-alcohol writers. I make a note to take a look at Goodwin's book, *Alcohol and the Writer.*

It is often quoted that of the seven earlier American writers who had won the Nobel prize – Sinclair Lewis, Eugene O'Neill, William Faulkner, Ernest Hemingway, Pearl Buck and Saul Bellow, only the last two weren't alcoholics. John Steinbeck, the seventh author, is usually listed as "drinking to excess" but manages to avoid being included along with the first four.

More recent American Nobel winners (Isaac Bashevis Singer, Czeslaw Milosz and Toni Morrison) all seem to have clean plates. Singer was a vocal vegetarian and is quoted as saying, "In relation to [animals], all people are Nazis; for the animals, it is an eternal Treblinka." I can't imagine he would be polluting his body with excess alcohol or drugs after that quote.

To round out my list of alcoholics, I add a few drug addicts – the classic opium addicts, Thomas De Quincey, Edgar Allan Poe, and the cooperative pair Charles Dickens and Wilkie Collins. Who would think of them as dipping into the opium to keep producing those weekly cliffhangers?

I know writers are more bipolar than the average population, but is their creativity a product of their disorder, or vice versa? Writers often seem eccentric, even to me, an eccentric writer myself. My oddities, however, seem mild when compared with most of the poets I meet. I can function at the Women's Institute meetings and can pass as ordinary in the supermarket aisles. It is true, I am very anxious that my book appear at its launch in time, but that is hardly odd. Nor is the obsessional way I tackle any editing that needs doing so strange. The obsession doesn't preclude me missing a few hanging participles and odd spellings.

Maybe the alcoholism is because writers have to work alone, and so are forced to confront their demons each time they sit down at the computer. The loneliness and the terrible gaps between one book and another are certainly challenging, as are negative reviews.

We don't keep alcohol in the house except for Bailey's Irish Cream, with which we celebrate my book contracts and Eli's sculpture sales by raising a very small liqueur glass of it in mutual appreciation of whatever creativity we have. Also, it is the most important ingredient in my rum balls. We don't drink coffee and rarely even herb teas. As to drugs? The island may, or may not, have its grow-houses, but my only experience with drugs was once, in Morocco, when I was given a cup of opium tea and woke with a colossal headache the next morning and no experience worth recording. "Once, with feeling" has always been a guiding principle for me in so many areas of my life.

I am a writer. How do I manage to maintain any kind of "high," and keep cheerful in the face of rejection? How do I keep a steady working level when all seems hopeless? I think it is because I have a curiosity about "what is to be on my next page," and also that I am willing to try new ideas even though they may lead away from sales. I very much like John Cage's quote, "I can't understand why people are frightened of new ideas. I'm frightened of old ones." While it is important to not throw the baby out with the bathwater, I feel it is also necessary to see beyond concepts and conditioning if one wants to come up with anything fresh that offers a creative approach to expressing the humanity and inhumanity of humankind.

A last note on alcoholism and writers – writers that keep going without getting lost in an alcoholic haze, usually have their own ways to maintain enough positive energy to continue. Twain used his friendship with Nikola Tesla to explore his scientific interests and actually took out three patents. This provided a nice balance for the witty, satirical image he continually seems to have had to present, both in his life and in his writings. Being funny all the while is often the defence mechanism of a depressed personality. Pearl Buck established Welcome House, the first international, interracial adoption agency, which channelled a certain amount of her energies. Moreover,

Ms. Buck came from a missionary family – although that doesn't necessarily ensure abstinence in the offspring. Saul Bellow had his love of the Bible to keep him on an even keel. I suppose his five wives could have easily driven him to drink, but they don't appear to have done so.

Twyla Tharp said, "Art is the only way to run away without leaving home," so perhaps instead of running away into alcohol and drugs, Eli and I just run away into sculpture and essays. It seems so much less trouble.

# April

There is nothing quite like spring cleaning to freshen one's spirits, so that is what I am doing this month. While changing winter-weight quilts to summer quilts, I remembered that a few years back I read fifteen John le Carré books, one after another, while making a wild quilt. I had recorded the experience somewhere, so looked up my notes and found a nice little piece on his books and my quilt.

### John le Carré and My Quilt

I have just discovered John le Carré; nearly fifty years after his first book came out. It is an awkward time in my life to have discovered him as I find his books very addictive, for I am scheduled to finish a quilt before the Island Open House in October.

Quilts, particularly patchwork quilts, are central to my life, which has itself been something of a pastiche (to put it politely) or, more accurately, hodgepodge. Still, to paraphrase from that very wonderful book by Rohinton Mistry, *A Fine Balance* (itself with a quilt theme), one cannot tell how the quilt will turn out until the last piece is in place. So I am anxious to finish the one I am working on. For someone like myself, who loves instantaneous results, quilting is a dreadful lesson in patience.

Life is a matter of balance, and so to solve the problem of the desire to withdraw and read all that le Carré has written at one sitting, with the need to finish the ridiculously enormous task of making a quilt, I have allowed myself one chapter to one piece of embroidery. Being both the slave and the slave-driver, I at once cheat and read two chapters, and sometimes three, before going into the studio to pick up my needle and thread.

This particular quilt is itself a double reflector of discarded fragments since it is not only made up entirely of begged or cast-off materials, but its theme is gypsies, partly because they too are rejected (as my quilt patches), but also because I, as a one-time flamenco aficionado, know that flamenco's roots among the gypsies were colourful and so match my bright-hued quilt. I usually connect a poem to each of my creations so here is the poem for the quilt:

**Gypsies**
I was seven or maybe eight
when I went with my father
to see the drifting gypsies.
My memories are a jumble of
clothespins and tinkered-kettles,
stolen apples in our pockets,
and a strange excitement
that I didn't yet recognize.
Something still lingers of that day;

clear as a fall morning
snatched from right and wrong;
and that's the feel of my small hand
in his as we walked together,
each seeking, in our own way,
an imagined freedom,
through the laden orchards
to their campsite.

My daughter, Beverly, tells me (if I heard her correctly) that it is dated and politically incorrect to write in such a romantic way about the gypsies. She is a wise woman and probably right. However it is my poem, and my childhood, so the poem stays and goes with the quilt when the quilt goes.

Since I feel that things fall into place when the time is right, I was amused when on our weekly trip to the island recycling centre, Eli picked up a recent *New Yorker* with an article in it on none other than John le Carré. The recycling centre is where I sometimes find cast-off bits of material to incorporate in my quilts, the *New Yorker* was itself being recycled and so I read the article with a view to how John le Carré might be recycling himself, as we all have to from time to time.

In the *New Yorker* article they write that le Carré's central theme is betrayal, but his works seem to me to concern themselves much more with roles and role-playing. His spies and spy-catchers turn at the wink of an eye from good guy to bad guy. One role peels off after another, until one wonders what is at the core. Le Carré never chooses (or maybe doesn't know how) to reveal this core. A spy's very training necessitates the adoption of a fresh persona complete in its minutiae. In my favourite John le Carré book, *The Little Drummer Girl* (which I mentioned earlier in the year), the spy-trainer chooses an actress for his joe (his running agent) and, in perhaps the most subtly erotic pages I have read recently, he moulds her into a woman in love with a terrorist/freedom fighter and she, confusing her roles, falls in love with both the trainer and the terrorist/freedom fighter she has yet to meet. This makes her a perfect double agent as she betrays first one, then the other.

I think betraying, which the *New Yorker* article accentuates, is merely choosing to adopt another role. Yet though the article talks of everyone being betrayed by someone, it does not mention the possibility of betraying oneself, one's true role, one's core. That may be the problem that John le Carré is wrestling with. It is certainly mine.

I am musing on this role-playing, and what my role really is, as I place an orange satin piece next to some drab red cotton and join them together with a chevron stitch in purple. The first memory coming up is of my father yelling at my mother (during one of their periodic rows), "You should have gone on the stage, Bob. You should have gone on the stage!" Bob was my mother's nickname. It is trite to think of this world as a stage, but recently I have come to think of myself as acting a series of roles, each played rather badly. I fluff my lines and am unsatisfactory with details, even though le Carré makes it clear that it is details that count. I am surprised that I have survived in such great style, since I have been so inadequate in the roles of scholar, wife, mother, therapist and artist. Maybe I am doing a sampling of roles this time around, just as I am sampling the piles of material in my studio and choosing the most appropriate and pleasing from them for the quilt. Or maybe my role is survivor, the closest to my genes' demands, and the one that seems to fit best.

The mood created by the softening of edges, as the masque proceeds in each of le Carré's books, makes the distinctions between male/female, hunter/hunted, good/bad, freedom fighter/terrorist seem primitive and limiting; just as in my quilt oranges shade into pinks and reds into purples. Such diffusion creates a certain unease in me, however, and I am anxious to define each colour, and so have chosen to outline each patch in a contrasting embroidery stitch. The prevailing colour in le Carré's early books is grey – grey ties, grey suits, grey faces, grey London, grey Bonn, all lost in a grey mist. It is as if his books were written in the land of the *pretas,* the hungry ghosts, who are condemned to search forever for a rebirth place they can never find.

However I, for the moment, have found a place of rebirth, and it is here, midst the meadow of oranges and mauves and pinks of my quilt. As I move on to placing a yellow bit of crepe up against a piece from some old floral drapes, I choose a shocking pink thread to join them in a maidenhair stitch. Still the le Carré books circulate through my system, and I find myself smiling gently as I wander dreamily among his grey cities along with his undercover agents and, at the same time, wonder who will lie under the covering of my finished quilt.

/lⴴl\

Well the quilts are changed, the corners are dusted (some for the first time in thirteen years) and I'm ready to rush out into the garden. Already the peas are up, and the rows of green garlic stems mark where I had planted the bulbs last October. I have spent a good part of the winter slipping in the odd garden-book reading, just to keep my spirits up in the hopes our harvest will be good this year.

"Don't wear perfume in the garden – unless you want to be pollinated by bees." So says Anne Raver, and people who demand that garden writing be in small, sexy bites could hardly ask for better than this. I feel the main problem with garden writing is not its lack of sexiness, but in how to cover the basics for the continually arriving new gardeners, while at the same time approaching topics in a fresh way and with recent scientific input for the advanced gardener. Of course, the author should do all this while keeping the reader on side, if not totally entranced. There is so much free information on the web as regards the pruning of roses etc., that garden writers need a certain slant, a particular niche, in order to attract attention. Above all there has to be passion in the writing and an ability to seduce the reader into this passion.

For myself, I can get any gardening "how-to" I need to know through Google. And anyway, when it comes to details for gardeners such as me, as Des Kennedy points out, "A few grains of information are seldom sufficient to derail instinct under a full head of steam." So for garden writing I lean to literary efforts.

I love Jamaica Kincaid's garden writing, with her feisty opinions and lackadaisical gardening style. She doesn't tell you how to do anything. In fact, she's probably a good example of "how not to garden" as she loses tools in the compost and orders masses of plants that all arrive on the same day with no ground prepared for them. She states her own garden-writing preference when describing a book by Sally Festing on Gertrude Jekyll. Of this book, she says, "This book is very decent and discreet – just the qualities I want in a friend, but not in a book I am reading." Her own garden books are full of gossip and asides. Her philosophy is very attractive – "People who know exactly what they are doing, always end up with exactly what they are doing." Her writing is shaped by her past, as her ancestors were brought over as slaves to Antigua to work the rubber plantations and so her prose has a definite passion and direction to it. There is no gardening aspect that Ms. Kincaid can't compare, contrast or parallel with the injustice of her slave ancestry. She describes this consciousness so clearly, "Should it be an idea; should it be an open wound, each breath I take in and expel healing and opening the wound again, over and over, or is it a long moment that begins anew each day since 1492?" Startling if you are just searching for how to prune your roses, but as you must know by now, I am not a gardener, or reader, who just wants information. The beginning of her *My Garden (Book)* could be described as a hybrid of Gertrude Stein and an upscale gardening catalogue as her much repeated phrases are punctuated with Latin names for plants. In spite of this, her vitality is irresistible and her enthusiasm will sweep you away.

Anne Raver, she of the sexy quote, is a brilliant garden writer for the *New York Times,* who uses the garden essay form the way I like it. "You can write about love, as sphinx moths visit the evening primroses opening up at dusk and bats swoop in to sip nectar from the saguaro cactus. You can write about death as the soldier bug prongs a Mexican beetle lunching on a leaf..." As you can see, she hangs any topic she wants into the frame of gardens.

There is also Rosemary Verey, who was the doyenne of English garden writers. Anne Raver describes Verey's books as "not only filled with countless ideas and how-tos but her delightful references to early garden literature also serve as a kind of joyful syllabus for self-education." I tried Verey's *The Garden in Winter,* and found it quite wonderful.

And speaking of early garden references, I came across a curious book the other day that surveys a whole slew of early garden writers, from pioneer/settler gardeners, to those of ladies accompanying their lordships to various short-term colonial postings, to writers on "railway-station gardens," writers pleading for "quiet Sundays," to modern magazine writers promoting self-sufficiency (a replay of pioneer gardens) so that we might all make a smaller ecological footprint. The collection is called *Garden Voices: Two Centuries of Canadian Garden Writing* and is a survey of Canadian garden writing. The couple who have researched and gathered these interesting pieces of writing together are Edwinna von Baeyer and Pleasance Crawford, perfect names that one might indeed have conjured up for garden writers appearing in a piece of fiction. Some quotes from their book include Carole Giangrande's "a garden feels like a victory, ground gained against a sense of widespread social chaos that has begun to feel like a norm." Carole was a CBC radio gardening personality in the '80s. I also very much like her quote that makes gardening almost a political statement, "this is why gardening is not only political but subversive: nothing works like people who quietly assert their power to reclaim their humanness, beginning with understanding how to feed themselves well. Politics begins with a garden. No one can live, yet alone protest, on an empty stomach." I love fresh approaches and claims for justifying something we enjoy doing anyway. Another writer in this collection is Roscoe A. Fillmore, who tells the new suburbanites of his time to "get their hands into the mud and never mind the rubber gloves," and adds, "And please do not do this just to keep up with the Joneses."

Another unusual book on gardening that I keep on my shelf of all-time favourites is rather rare. I managed to get its tenth impression, which is dated 1939. It is the witty garden writing classic by Karel Čapek, *The Gardener's Year.* I am particularly fond of the account he gives in it of a gardener who decides to go away on holiday in August and so asks his neighbour to pop over occasionally to check things out. In anxiety, each day he is away he sends more and more detailed instructions for the neighbour. Of course the neighbour is overloaded and fails miserably. On returning to a ruined garden, our gardener vows never to do such a foolish thing again. Another of Čapek's essays concerns itself with how a gardener buys up a whole lot of plants for a vacant patch of earth only to find, on the first spade dig, that he has "forced out a mass of roots, on top of which a whole clump of buds is clustered. 'God, Almighty!' moans the gardener, 'I've got trollius here.'" It is brilliant writing and holds a good moral ... if you start a garden, you'd better stay with it. I think it's worth trying Amazon for this one.

**/IL⚠I\**

I've just been reading a manuscript someone has written on literacy. It is tedious and dull and wouldn't get me off the couch to even order the book from the library should it ever find a publisher. Meanwhile, I have recently finished two other books that can only encourage one to rush out to the nearest library, so enthusiastic are they about the ability and opportunity to read. Both books certainly had me making lists of future reading material with gusto. The books are minor, but each is wonderful in its own way. The first is the slender novel by Dai Sijie called *Balzac and the Little Chinese Seamstress.* The two young men in this novel have barely received any kind of an education, but since they came from professional families, they were cast into the Chinese wilderness at the time of the cultural revolution, when the idea was that intellectuals should have their lives balanced out by manual labour in the country. I have often thought that the intellectual needs manual work as a nice balance for a mind that could easily go out of kilter, but the Cultural Revolution was not the way to go about putting this into practice and it wasted millions of what could have otherwise been useful lives – a whole generation in fact.

The boys, in the story, meet a third young man who secretly has a trunk of forbidden books hidden away. How they get their hands on these books and how they seduce the pretty little seamstress with promises of Balzac is the gist of the story. This is a book to make readers of us all, for it accentuates the preciousness of books when they are forbidden and the cherishing of each word as the books are read aloud and discussed in great earnestness. Often we have to be deprived of something in order to realize its value and in this charming little novel, books are the heroes and the golden grail. If it doesn't make you enthused about your local library, I don't know what will. By the way, it's not a spoiling of the ending, but the little seamstress does not get hooked on reading, still the books involved do inspire her to ... well I won't spoil it for you; read this charming novella for yourself.

The second book that in its own eccentric way also encourages reading needs a bit of an introduction. My mother, in useless anxiety that they would not arrive in time, always sent her gifts weeks before the birthday or holiday for which they were intended, and my twin contin- ues that practice, for I received her last Xmas gifts in November. However this time she gets points, for along with two bottles of Givenchy perfume (perfume is frowned upon on the island so I feel secretly wicked when I put a drop behind each ear as I load the washing machine), she sent a wonderful book, *The Uncommon Reader* by Alan Bennett. Alan Bennett is accused of cosy writing. Well if this is so, I pray to be able to write cosily every day. It is a brilliantly funny political satire about how the Queen gets hooked on books. As with every good book I read, I tell the next hundred people I meet about it. A friend of mine is very sick, and so I ask her husband to get it for her from the library. When he looks for it, there are fifty folk reserv- ing the title ahead of him. I have a heated discussion with myself, but eventually my better part wins and I dispatch my copy to her. It is not an act of generosity because the pause between the impulse and the act was too long. Once at a party I admired someone's necklace. The owner took it off and put it around my neck. I have always wanted to do something like that, but have rarely pulled it off. Yet this time giving was rewarded by receiving, for I was given a second copy of *The Uncommon Reader* for Xmas and so have a copy in the house for reading when I occasionally feel the world isn't going the way it should.

As I mentioned, *The Uncommon Reader* tells how the Queen gets hooked on books. The Royal family, as we all know, is not a hothouse of culture, so this charming account of a wilful Queen is totally entrancing. I just loved it when, in the middle of a Henry James tome, she mutters, "Oh do get on!" The Queen decides to have a soiree, in which she actually meets her favourite authors; it is not, as to be expected, successful. She feels "they are probably best met in the pages of their novels," and were as much creatures of the reader's imagination as the characters in their books. Though having had a very different upbringing, the Puritan element in mine reflects her Majesty's, for when asked "how far did you read?" she replies, "Oh to the end. Once I start a book I finish it. That was the way one was brought up. Books, bread and butter, mashed potatoes, one finishes what is on one's plate." Yes, one does. Read this book, share it, steal it, donate it … this is the kind of book to get folks reading.

I actually ordered some of the Queen's reading list, but gave up fairly quickly and can only admire the old girl for hanging in through Ivy Compton-Burnett and the others.

Recently we saw a DVD on Windsor Castle and, while the logistics are daunting (and the fact that two people need one hundred and fifty servants is somewhat appalling), still what alternative is there? Even if the Queen and Prince Philip retired and went into seniors' housing, what could happen to Windsor? It would only be made into a luxury hotel and spa for other wasteful and arrogant wealthy people. She might as well stay there. The corgis love it anyway.

A last word on literacy. I'm not sure who wrote about "the humanizing nature of literature," and I know that many terrible deeds have been done by literate folk; still, I'd opt for literacy over illiteracy any day when it comes to the opening of possibilities and the releasing of potentials.

ⅢⱭⅠ\

My reading of *The Tale of Genji* is now up to page eight hundred. I'm definitely settling down with it. As I mentioned, this is the brilliant Royall Tyler translation. I used to read a former and somewhat briefer translation of this book, by Edward G. Seidensticker, every Xmas, and even wrote a poem about this unusual choice for my holiday reading:

### On the Annual Reading of Genji Monogatari at Christmastime

Last year I didn't read *Genji*,
although for the previous
ten Christmases I had. Perhaps
I was feeling like tempting fate
after an unusually good year.
This year again I pick it up
at that time, for me, of sorrows,
when the first decorations
appear in the stores and
Santa costumes are taken out
and aired yet once more.
So yet once more I read that
also tale of sorrows; of life
too wretched to endure and yet
too sweet to entirely give up.

# ⅡⅬⅅⅠ\

I broke into the tanka world last year with beginner's luck. It happened this way. Sonja Arntzen, the Japanese medieval literature authority whom I mentioned earlier, was willing to give some tanka-writing workshops, which I enthusiastically attended. I fell in love with this poetry form, and, on submitting some of my early and tentative efforts, I found my tanka accepted in some fine journals alongside some really splendid and well-established tanka writers.

I should mention that traditional Japanese tanka is made up of five lines of 5, 7, 5, 7 and 7 syllables. Adding those two extra lines to a haiku's length gave me permission to also add emotions and ideas to my writing, for haiku are recordings of the senses only – no metaphors, similes, emotions or ideas directly expressed. Writing tanka made me feel like an imago emerged from its pupa. Tanka is one of the earliest forms of poetry in Japan and although my Japanophilia has waned somewhat since my stay there in the 80s, this element of Japanese culture still resonates strongly within my being. I had wanted to go to Japan ever since I was two years old, when I had insisted (to the point of temper tantrum) on wearing kimono and *geta* for a fancy-dress party. Having succeeded in going, I have now tried for the last twenty years to expunge "things Japanese" from my life in order to explore new territory, but I have not been successful.

My attachment to Japan and my love of curious people combine in, say, someone like Lafcadio Hearn, an unusual American (well actually he was born on an Ionian isle and was brought up in Ireland, but moved to America when he was nineteen), who arrived in Japan at the end of the nineteenth century. Hearn stayed there, married a Japanese woman and eventually was allowed to take up Japanese citizenship, which at that time required him to change his name. So he did, to Koizumi Yakumo.

I love his story about the *Daruma* and will try to retell it now:

Lafcadio Hearn went one summer to a little fishing village, so small that there was no hotel. He stayed above a fish shop, that being the only accommodation available, and had wonderful fish meals during his stay.

One day he noticed a *kamidana* (Shinto shrine shelf) at the back of the shop, and under the shelf, another smaller shelf with a red Daruma, a good luck charm, on it. A Daruma is a legless figure, weighted, so that when it is pushed over, it comes springing back up. A good reminder to bounce back after adversity. When bought, the Daruma is eyeless. In front of the Daruma on the shelf was an offering of food. The Daruma had only one eye painted on.

Hearn asked the owner why the Daruma only had one eye. "Well," the owner replied, "I had a great day fishing earlier in the year so I gave him one eye in thanks."

Hearn then asked him why he wouldn't give the Daruma two eyes for he looked so unhappy with only one eye. The owner responded by saying that when he had a day of equally good fortune he would then paint in the other eye.

The night before Lafcadio Hearn finished his holiday, he asked the shopkeeper for his bill. It was for a very modest amount. Hearn had had such a great time that he doubled the amount on paying.

The next morning he got up early to prepare for departure. A splendid breakfast was ready for him. As he drank his last bowl of miso soup, he glanced towards the kamidana with its candles burning for the household kami (spirit). Suddenly he noticed the Daruma on the shelf below also had a candle burning in front of it. The Daruma looked back at Lafcadio Hearn with two eyes.

Now please don't ask me why I love things Japanese!

Lafcadio Hearn is especially well-known for his collections of Japanese legends and ghost stories, such as *Kwaidan: stories and studies of strange things.*

Oh dear! I knew speaking about Hearn would get me going again, for here's another Japanese book in my book-box. I am not a "catty" kind of person (in the animal-owner sense, that is), but I have just been reading a very charming book that might, perhaps, allow me another take on those furry pets. It is Sōseki Natsume's *I am a Cat.* This charming book, an early twentieth-century Japanese classic, is about a wise and wonderful cat who, on overhearing human discussions and watching human behaviour, comments caustically and wittily on the Japanese upper-middle-class of that time. This cat was born world-weary. The novel was serialised in *Hototogisu,* a magazine founded by Shiki as a haiku magazine, which later changed to accept general literary pieces. It is Aiko Ito and Graeme Wilson's version of *I am a Cat* that I am reading.

The cat in the story comments on the straightforward-ness of "catness" when compared with the complexity of human motivation – "If we want to eat, we eat; if we want to sleep, we sleep; when we are angry, we are angry utterly; when we cry, we cry with all the desperation of extreme commitment to our grief." Further to this, the cat comments on the protagonist keeping a diary, "Thus we [cats] never keep things like diaries. What would be the point? We live our diaries and consequently have no need to keep a daily record as a means of maintaining our real character."

The commentator in this book reminds me somewhat of Mehitabel in Don Marquis' *Archy and Mehitabel.* Archy is a loveable cockroach, who hammers his diary out with his head on an ancient typewriter's keys (thus never being able to use capitals), and his wonderful friend, Mehitabel, is an alley cat and the reincarnation of Cleopatra. Though also world-weary, or rather world-worn-out, Mehitabel manages to keep remarkably cheerful and her *"toujours gai, toujours gai"* often rings out in some of my darker moments to remind me to keep my spirits up.

# May

The rain has ceased activity, but I haven't, for I am wildly running back and forth from the propagation box to the veggie patch planting out my seedlings. I'm also protecting my pea-shoots from the marauding robins and doing a cleanup of piles of cuttings that I had neglected to do in the fall. I have almost no time for reading. Please note that I said "almost," for it would be a doubly blue moon before I could resist my overflowing book-box, which at the moment seems filled with tempting library books. This always seems to happen when my domestic duties demand my attention be elsewhere.

I rarely buy new books. I have a running list at a couple of second-hand bookstores for odd titles that I seem to need desperately, although I can't quite remember why. Sometimes, however, I come across a library book that I would like to buy so that I could have it available around the house, to dip into it from time to time, and there is one such book in my book-box right now. It is *The Book of Numbers: The Secret of Numbers and How They Changed the World* by Peter J. Bentley, and that is just what it is, a book about numbers and number theory, from the first notches a hunter might have made in a stick to indicate deer killed, to the fascinating patterns of Mandelbrot Sets. The book is attractively illustrated and could easily be considered a coffee-table book. I always start such large books full of hope that they will engross me and focus my scattered energies for a while. This time I reach page forty-eight, still glorying in numbers, which I feel hold the secret to everything. Alas, on this page the editor has not caught Mr. Bentley's (or his proofreader's) error in saying that nine is a prime number and my little heart drops to the bottom of wherever it can drop. It is like finding the first fault in a lover that marks the end of the honeymoon. Yet I carry on bravely with Mr. Bentley because I have never yet found a book that hasn't at least one blooper, but this is rather a big one, I must admit.

This book is a beautifully presented history of mathematics, and, despite the errors (including a misspelling of "mathematics" in one place), it is still a great introduction to number theory. You can go elsewhere should you want to pursue any of the topics, such as Mandelbrot Sets, at greater length (and with perhaps more accuracy). The book also includes some wonderful photos of these mysterious Mandelbrot Sets.

When I finished *The Book of Numbers,* I forgave Mr. Bentley the errors since he had given me a great quote by John von Neumann, "If people do not believe that mathematics is simple, it is only because they do not realize how complicated life is." Also, I should mention that *The Book of Numbers* provides what most mathematicians consider the most beautiful equation in the world. Mistakes, or not, go read it for its exposition on Euler's equation:

$$e^{i\pi} + 1 = 0$$

# ᚾᛁᛑᛁᚾ

*The Book of Numbers* was fairly hard going and demanded a certain concentration, but my second book for May, Cynthia Ozick's book of literary criticism, *The Din in the Head,* is definitely way over mine. However I do sift out a few gems, "Some matters are, in truth, more urgent, and significant, than others." I wonder which she would choose – genocide over the latest skirt length would be a certainty, but after that? I suddenly remember the days when I was pushing my first husband to be a major artist. I mixed with couples patronizing the arts and recall one scene when one of the wives had not been accepted into the inner circle of art patrons. Her sorrow and raging were dramatic. I thought at the time that her intense pain at being rejected could be compared to a daughter being shunned by the family. So how does one rate significant matters, I wonder?

I am a wondering kind of person, so I proceed to wonder what kind of literary essay Ms. Ozick would write about my own writing. Would she say, as she did for Updike, "[Wakan] reconciles the social bustle of ordinary lives with the rapturous aloneness of faith?" No, she wouldn't say that, because my faith is indeterminate, although I know plenty about social bustle and loneliness. Still her point that "the life of crowds snuffs the mind's murmurings," is well taken and I will try earnestly to cut back on our little island's wild social life.

Ms. Ozick would not view my own book-notes as any kind of serious literary criticism, and I would agree with her. I am neither academically trained in the field, nor am I rigorous in my analysis of plot or style. What can serious literary criticism provide for the general reader, I wonder? And, when I wonder, I make lists:

- It can set the book in context, e.g., knowing the times in which a book was written might better explain the content and language.
- It can point out which side of an argument the book is presenting, and possibly present a balancing view.
- It can help us decide whether a book is worth reading, will be of interest to us and whether it is of value to humanity.
- It can present a background of the author's life that might explain why the book was written, though some critics prefer to stay with the merits of the written text alone. Still, providing information about where the author is coming from might enrich our reading.
- It can point out moral lessons – indicate the seriousness of the intent of the author and how we can profit from his/her message. I usually prefer to work this out for myself, not denying I can profit from the reading, but liking to think I can decide for myself how I should profit.
- It can point out the trueness or falseness with which humanity or a certain situation is presented.

- Literary critics belonging to a certain interest group would approach the text for example from a feminist viewpoint, or perhaps a gay one. For groups that are under-represented, this serves a useful political function.

Some literary criticism concentrates on the language of the work alone – the use of metaphor, irony, etc. This kind of criticism often downplays the setting of the book, its position in our culture and the foibles of the author.

I mentioned earlier how Frances Duncan's novel, *Dragonhunt,* was a Jungian novel. Sometimes literary critics analyze the book from the point of view of a certain school of psychology, for instance Freudian (Oedipus complex), Jungian (individuation), Adlerian (power struggles). To expand this idea, a Jungian critic would go for the jugular (I nearly wrote jungular) of the archetypes in the book (the innocent hero, the wise man, the crone) and the spiritual journey towards the Holy Grail and completeness. A good example of a strong Jungian slant is Bettina L. Knapp's book, *The Brontës: Branwell, Anne, Emily, Charlotte.*

As I learned many years ago in my first year psychology class, "Perception is functionally selective." So select your literary critic, but be aware that they always come with their own biases.

As for myself, I am not, I'm afraid, an analytical literary critic, nor, indeed, a very erudite commentator. I am just the average obsessive reader, but one who has set herself the task of getting other people as excited about books as I am; to inform about their power to enrich one's life, and to tell about the privilege they bestow on the reader of being able to communicate with great ideas and with people who are skilful observers of the world about them. I feel somewhat like an evangelical preacher as I tell folk how a few well-chosen words can give a lift to one's spirit (through laughter or through tears) to a plane where the things of the everyday world seem to weave together in some meaningful way. I'm afraid a certain pomposity goes with the territory of evangelism, so I usually follow up my exhortations with some kind of pratfall – a gross misinter-pretation of a text, or an ill-informed literary judgement – to show that the messenger bearing good news can some-times be a clown.

In Cynthia Ozick's piece on Isaac Babel, I duly record his quote, "No iron spike can pierce a human heart as icily as a period in the right place." However, I am partial to the use of three dots myself, showing my hesitant nature and indicating that I never claim to know how things will turn out. For this reason, I prefer to leave some sentences open to many possibilities, hesitating to use the defining firm-ness of closure that a full-stop implies ...

ΙΙ⅃◢Ιⵣ

My hesitant nature often leads to a certain sloppiness with details I must admit, so I just sighed when a book I had ordered, turned out to be a children's book. The title had seemed promising, *Oak and Company* by Richard Mabey, and the contents even more intriguing as the history of an oak tree was going to be laid out. For some reason my circuitous mind had jumped to the conclusion that the history of the oak was going to be paralleled with the history of England during the period of the tree's growth. A nice conceit, I thought, and worthy of a couple of days of my time. The book was merely a history of an oak tree with all the relevant botanical facts presented without whimsy, and accompanied by rather charming paintings.

I read it in fifteen minutes and put it back on our library return shelf. It did, however, induce me to pull some books out from the children's book section of my own book collection and wax nostalgic for a few moments over the books that I had thought worth saving. They stemmed from the days when my husband and I had a small educational-book business called Pacific Rim Publishers, so most of the books I had in my arms were related to Japanese or Chinese themes. There was the wonderful tale, *Ming Lo Moves the Mountain* by Arnold Lobel, and my all-time favorite, *Crow Boy* by Taro Yashima; I defy you to read this one without your eyes watering up just a bit. It is the tale of a country boy who for five years walks across the fields to school. He is treated as an outcast by the village children and is teased and bullied, yet still he comes to school every day without missing one. In his graduation year, a new teacher comes to the school. He finds out that the boy knows a lot about wild plants and flowers and that he could draw them, and so the teacher uses this knowledge as a way to bond with the boy. At the graduation concert, the boy comes on stage and the children can't understand why. The teacher tells them that the boy will imitate the sounds of crows and the teacher explains how the boy had learned these from observing crows over all the years he has plodded back and forward to school. *Crow Boy* does this so beautifully that all the children start to cry thinking how wrongly they had treated him, and of course, I too am in tears by this time.

The next book I look at is the wry tale, *The Taoist Priest of Laoshan Mountain,* adapted by Cao Zuorui, a lesson to folks chasing after enlightenment, and another is the very relevant ecological story about *The Man who Planted Trees* by Jean Giono and translated by Peter Doyle. The last book I pulled out was the fun cartoon book, *What Do Authors Do?* by Eileen Christelow, which perhaps was one I carried in our catalogue for one student only, myself, for within a couple of years, I was a full-time writer and perhaps this book nudged me a little in that direction. All these books for children carried wise lessons for adults. Our customers were school boards, librarians and teachers, so I never found out whether children really liked them; but I do know that I described them so enthusiastically in our cata-logue that teachers certainly bought them by the box.

A few of the titles we carried made it on to Ministry of Education lists, but I never cared whether they did, or didn't, because I had hand-picked each title because it had swept me up and carried me away, even though it may only have been for a short time. But that is sometimes all one can ask of a book, isn't it?

**ⅡⅬ◢Ⅱ\**

Just finished Margaret MacMillan's excellent little book, *The Uses and Abuses of History.* Here's one book that I will re-read at least once a year. Don't borrow this one, buy it!

Now, have I asked you to do this before? You need this book to give you a broader perspective, to offer you a deeper understanding, to help you with not only humanity's past, but with your own. I consider this book, of a modest one hundred and eighty-seven pages, to be probably the most important (at least for me) in recent years, for it speaks of memory and lies and deceptions, and how history is rewritten, and how we each rewrite our own.

Consider this – when we remember any incident, don't we always betray it in some way – by omission, by addition, by slanting, by selection? History, and that includes personal history, is about what we choose to remember of the past and what we choose to forget. As Ms. MacMillan says, "The past can be used for almost anything you want to do in the present," meaning that the past can easily be twisted to justify present action, whether for good or bad. She adds, "memory is selective and malleable." And sums it up by pointing out that "we can draw our lessons [from the past] carefully or badly." She gives many examples of how nineteenth-century nationalism invented traditions and histories to justify the borders each country had chosen.

My niece collects the family past. I've never bothered with it myself, never registered on Friends Reunited. In fact as far as friends go, I've merely watch them drift away to do their own thing, wherever they have chosen to move, and I have just as quietly allowed others to drift into my sphere of current friendships. Even though I don't cling, I can meet up with long-moved-away friends years later and continue our discussion as if we'd merely stopped in mid-sentence.

From my past, I have one letter from my mother (not addressed to me), a few photos sent from my niece's collection and several pages of my mother's poetry. It appeared that no one in the family seemed to want the poetry as much as I did. The oldest artefact from my life is a Diamond Deb nail file that my husband romantically bought for me thirty years ago from Holt Renfrew. I am not attached to my history, though I may stoop to blame it when caught in an inexactitude in the present.

I take heed of Ms. MacMillan's advice in regards to history, "Use it, enjoy it, but always handle history with care." I haven't read any of her histories yet. Well, I did start her enormous prize-winning tome, *Paris 1919: Six Months That Changed the World,* but I didn't finish it, for I had other things on my mind at the time besides the Treaty of Versailles. Yet I am sure Ms. MacMillan prepares her books with great care; care for details, care for balanced opinions and care for getting as close to what really happened as possible. That woman has integrity, with a capital "I" and I write to tell her so.

**ILⱭI\**

When it comes to words, who can beat Peter Mark Roget, he of *Roget's Thesaurus?* I've just read *The Man Who Made Lists: Love, Death, Madness, and the Creation of "Roget's Thesaurus"* by Joshua Kendall and was fascinated to find it all came out of protection, that is from Roget protecting himself from an ever-present and intrusive mother. From an early age Roget withdrew into making lists and putting things into categories as a way of avoiding his mother's constant attentions. With a mad mother, a father who died when Roget was young and an uncle who actually committed suicide in his arms, lists became the way Roget made sense of his life. It was this protective mechanism that later brought him generations of renown.

As a child, the lists he would make were for the categorizing of plants, animals and abstract things. He kept these lists going throughout his life, eventually developing them into a thesaurus which became a bestseller. Even into his old age, Roget stayed clear-minded and categorizing; in his eighties he was still tinkering with new editions of the book.

Considering Roget's lists, I mused on what I used as a child as a defence mechanism from a crowded household and an ever-present twin. I remember telling my father, in a moment of childish anger, that he couldn't stop me thinking. So I guess I went on using my busy little brain to work out foolish things like what I should have said or done, that I hadn't, and clever things like connecting odd ideas for odd poems.

ﬡ𝗟𝘻ﬥﬡ

As one ages, death becomes more and more an intimate friend. However, two hundred and fifty pages about an intelligent man's fear of death is more than enough. *Nothing to be Frightened Of* by Julian Barnes is the book in question. If you are an ardent Christian you will expect to be greeted by Jesus and the disciples, if not God him/herself when you die. If a wobbly agnostic, at least the possibility of the odd relative turning up outside the golden gates is in the works. But what if you are an atheist and believe in nothing? Julian Barnes, once an atheist and now moved to an agnostic position, lets us know that people tell him that there is nothing to be afraid of, but, unfortunately, that is just what terrifies Mr. Barnes – nothing; that there should be nothing after death.

Even the most ardent believer has a few moments of terror as death approaches, but to have that terror for a lifetime and not do anything about it seems strange to me, but then I often have ridiculously easy solutions for most of the world's problems.

Mr. Barnes speaks of dreams of tunnels and I decide to write to him and tell him that the worst has probably already happened and that those tunnels are not after-death experiences, but actually a before-birth experience, for what is the birth canal but a tunnel? I hope Mr. Barnes will greet this piece of information I am offering him with a gigantic Zen laugh and a deep heave of relief. He may very well not.

What strikes me is how unprofitable (apart from the sales of his book about his fear) this dread has been all Mr. Barnes' life. Tragedy keeps us fixated at the navel level of our own ridiculousness. If he could only convert his fear into comedy, stretch it out to sweep in all mankind, Mr. Barnes would feel the weight lessen noticeably. I feel it is narcissistic to get stuck in one's own little life. The odds are that the separate self we fuss about is merely a moment in time, perhaps even just a segue between this universe and that universe. It is quite possible that when we examine "self" closely, this self we place so much importance on might dissolve into the very same nothingness that Mr. Barnes dreads so much.

Enough on death for a rainy afternoon on the west coast. Mr. Barnes is witty and erudite and scatters his text with quotes from his favourite French writers, and for those reasons alone his book is worth a speed-read. I think I would recommend that, as a writer, Mr. Barnes acquire a mortgage, I find it concentrates the energies so nicely. And having only one breast, perhaps I have the advantage over Mr. Barnes, since losing bits of your body slowly over the years does rather prepare you for what might very well be total annihilation.

ᴧⱽ

Rain continues, so it is pleasant to have spent a few days with two very satisfying books. Neither book is pretentious and that is their charm. The first is *Lark Rise* by Flora Thompson, a recalling of village life at the end of the nineteenth century. How can one have nostalgia for a time and place one never knew, I wonder, for the book totally draws me in with its detailed description of the lives of poverty-stricken villagers in a small hamlet. A poet, such as I, on a small pension and living on an idyllic little island could draw out some strands in common, I suppose. I just adore this book. Apparently it was made into a television series, but as I don't have a TV, I was luckily unaware of the fact and enjoyed the black words on paper as much as I have enjoyed any words on paper. Ms. Thompson has no axe to grind, just crystal-clear seeing and recording of a passing way of life.

The second book, *The Whole Five Feet: What the Great Books Taught Me About Life, Death, And Pretty Much Everything Else* by Christopher Beha, is brilliant. Mr. Beha suddenly decides to read all fifty books included in the five-foot shelf of Harvard Classics, assembled by Dr. Eliot one hundred years ago. Dr. Eliot, a past president of Harvard University, felt that in an age when only three percent of the population went to college, a person, by reading from the Classics that he had selected for fifteen minutes a day, could acquire in a few years what a higher education might offer.

Dr. Eliot states his purpose as follows, "My purpose in selecting the Harvard Classics was to provide the literary material from which a careful and persistent reader might gain a fair view of the progress of man observing, recording, inventing and imagining from the earliest historical times to the close of the nineteenth century."

Mr. Beha was fooling himself as he started, if he thought he was just reading five feet of books as some kind of educational achievement, for he gains so much more as he reads these carefully selected volumes. They help him recall moments in his grandmother's life, help him live through the death of a beloved aunt, help him re-examine his own devastating illness and help him begin to realise that the deep issues of life such as "what is the purpose of life?" and "how can we lead a good life?" have not changed over the years. He discovers in the texts, whether it be *Don Quixote* or Machiavelli's *The Prince,* quotes that he resonates with and that link past wisdom to present needs. As he says, "I was learning more about how to be in the world than I was any particular facts or figures." It was a clever idea of Mr. Beha to take on such a challenge, but more than that, *The Whole Five Feet* is a deeply moving record of a person's voyage into the past to give him courage to continue in the present. The reading of the books, rather than working as a withdrawal, actually kept "sending him back into the world."

He sums up the reading of the Harvard Classics, which took him a year, by saying "But these books have helped me to find meaning in events – illness and loss as well as moments of great joy – that didn't make any sense to me. At the same time, life helped me to make sense of these books. And so it will continue to go, for although I have read through the whole five feet, I'll never be finished with them."

The writings chosen by Dr. Eliot were grouped together by period or by style, e.g., the Greek dramatists all went together and Aesop was gathered along with the other tellers of fables. Here is what went into Volume 18, which was Modern English Drama:

*All for Love* by John Dryden
*The School for Scandal* by Richard Brinsley Sheridan
*She Stoops to Conquer* by Oliver Goldsmith
*The Cenci* by Percy Bysshe Shelley
*A Blot in the 'Scutcheon* by Robert Browning
*Manfred* by Lord Byron

And Volume 38: HARVEY, JENNER, LISTER, PASTEUR

*The Oath of Hippocrates*
*Journeys in Diverse Places* by Ambroise Paré
*On the Motion of the Heart and Blood in Animals* by William Harvey
*The Three Original Publications on Vaccination Against Smallpox* by Edward Jenner
*The Contagiousness of Puerperal Fever* by Oliver Wendell Holmes
*On the Antiseptic Principle of the Practice of Surgery* by Joseph Lister
Scientific Papers by Louis Pasteur
Scientific Papers by Charles Lyell

I'm glad to see that this last list starts with the Hippocratic oath, an oath I thought was framed in every doctor's office, along with their degrees, but all I seem to see there these days is a notice declaring that they are only willing to deal with one complaint at a time, as if the body is somehow disconnected into a hundred parts.

As the *New York Times* puts it about this modest but wonderful book, "Life intruded rudely on Beha's sabbatical, and he rose to the occasion by writing an unexpected narrative that deftly reconciles lofty thoughts and earthy pain. In doing so, he makes an elegant case for literature as an everyday companion no less valuable than the iPod."

I sigh gently after reading these two books, for both are totally unpretentious, disarming and real.

I finish the month with a novel. Occasionally, like the two books that I have just written about, a book is satisfactory without question – one dwells on every word of the book, and, when it is finished, puts it on one's shelf of to-be- read-again-someday books. This is the case with *Suite Française* by Irène Némirovsky. "Stunning," "Superb," "tour de force," use whatever words come to mind for this miraculous portrayal of war, wartime occupation and a gentle love that can penetrate through greed and corruption, and which lingers with the reader long after the book is closed. The author died in Auschwitz concentration camp and her daughters carried the manuscript around for years before this wonderful book eventually found its way into print.

As merely an historical document of the exodus from Paris after the German invasion of 1940, and of life, in France, under the Nazi occupation, *Suite Française* would be remarkable, but add to this a gentle, impossible love story, and you have a book that will outlast a generation. There are so few of these coming out of the publishing mill these days, I feel.

For my Genji followers, I am now nearing the end of *The Tale of Genji.* In former readings, my interest had always lagged after Genji dies (around page eight hundred in this translation), but the translator has captured the essence of the Heian court so well, that I feel I have almost entered into *The Tale of Genji* myself, wearing my twelve layers of kimono with my long, polished, black hair moving gently with the hem of the outer one, and so I feel I can willingly pursue the book to its end. Genji, that perfect lover, fine poet and musician, and almost perfect man (except for a major cuckolding incident, which you only have to read the first three hundred pages to explore) often threatened to leave the transitory world of the court, take up monk's robes and seek the eternal. He whined about this a lot (even superheroes can whine) but never did withdraw into a monastery.

*The Tale of Genji* is dense with Buddhist ideas, particularly the notion that suffering is caused by attachment. Attached as Genji is to life at the court and to his women, he realises that everything must pass. This I tell myself also from time to time and I can't protect myself from the sadness that arises when I do, no matter how I wrap it in mundane and domestic matters. This inevitability that all things must pass hit me recently, when, taking down a frequently-read poetry book, it fell to pieces – page by page to the floor. Much impressed by the significance of this, I wrote a small poem on the ephemeralness of all things.

### 15 Canadian Loose-leaf Poets

Seeking solace from the weary world,
I take *15 Canadian Poets* gently from its shelf.
Not gently enough, apparently,
for as I open the pages, I hear
the spine crack, and watch bemused as
15 Canadian poets float page by page to the floor.
Quick there's Atwood's *Game after Supper,*
surely such nostalgia deserves a firmer gluing.
And there's Bowering's *Triple Birth*
getting a fourth and see how Cohen
settles his *worshipped wounds and relics*
so heavily on Layton's *Fertile Muck.*
Avison's *The Swimmer's Moment* whirlpools to the floor

as Coleman's *The Lady Vanishes* disappears below
Jone's *Beautiful Creatures Brief As These.*
MacEwen's pages escape the cover as easily as
her *Manzini's handcuff tricks* and what more can be said
as Ondaatje's *For John, Falling,* does so?
Newlove's *The Arrival* has departed and
Nowlan's *Beginning* ends on the carpet.
Purdy's *Transient* is sic gloria and Mandel,
even as he tumbles, remembers Auschwitz.
Of all, only Birney sticks obstinately to the cover,
on which 15 Canadian poets mostly glower at me
in their photographic medallions.
Souster, on the bottom right, wearing a white shirt
and tie, is looking meek (or is it sullen?), anyway
he seems to be making some last-stand
Canadian statement.

# June

The garden is almost out of control with its thrustings-up and buddings and flowerings. It is overwhelming me with its fecundity. I turn to GIRO (Gabriola Island Recycling Depot) for some relief-reading, and manage to pick up a copy of *The Rainbow* by D. H. Lawrence. It turns out not to be the light summer reading that I was seeking. I am, however, captivated and amazed at his perceptive and sensitive description of human feelings, particularly those revolving around love and the sexual act. It is breathtaking how he can speak of men or women equally well in this way. He views their relationship as a power struggle, it is true, when that is only one aspect of a multi-layered association, but he does it so well.

Lawrence's *Lady Chatterley's Lover* is on my favourites' shelf and, while *The Rainbow* doesn't quite come up to it in some ways, it exceeds it in others, so I've decided to start a collection of Lawrence's works.

Here's a poem I jotted down after my umpteenth reading of *Lady Chatterley.*

### Lady Chatterley's Chores
And when she is not
occupied, threading
flowers in her lover's
pubic hair, does

my Lady Chatterley
peer with him into
a blocked drain
wondering whether
some wildlife hasn't
found refuge there,
or gape into a washing machine
that seems to be grinding
up clothes, or gawk into
the septic tank that appears
to have disconnected itself
from the house's toilets?
Lady Chatterley, and her lover, pondering
how to solve the everyday problems
of their sensual home.

## ᴨᴧᴎ

I am preparing for the annual haiku meet at Drumbeg House Studio in July. At the moment, the situation at our home is the following: a house is to be barged on next door (an old house brought over by barge from Vancouver); a well is being dug (pounded, actually) across the road with its persistent banging for days on end, which means there is a very real possibility that our well-water supply may fail, and toilets will be unavailable when twenty-five haiku poets arrive; and the stove and fridge are about to give up the ghost. I settle down with *Women in Love.* What else is there to do?

D. H.'s characters do fret about themselves a lot. Even the most elementary of farmers seems to spend more time in self-reflection than he does on his cattle. And, when relationships are in full swing, there's no holding D. H.

back as his men and women and men and men and women and women spend hours analysing their feelings and where the feelings might be taking them even as they are going that way. The results, as in *Women in Love,* are mostly grim. Where they are not total disasters, there is always a feeling of incompleteness, so that one partner is left desolate, even though the relationship is sealed. The other is left feeling guilty forever for the missing qualities they could not provide.

Still on the subject of relationships and the hard work involved in maintaining one, I am fascinated to read that Geoffrey Miller has worked out that it takes one million words of courtship before a baby is conceived. I forget the page on which he speaks of this in his fascinating book, *The Mating Mind: How Sexual Choice Shaped the Evolution of Human Nature,* but it's worth ploughing through the whole thing just to find this exposition. He calls it the million-word hurdle and even the most strong and silent of us are willing to go through it in order to have our genes continue.

Still buried in Miller's book, I read where he defines "consciousness" as "that treacherous patch of philosophi-cal quicksand." As I have declared that this is the year I'm going to explore the link between the brain and conscious-ness, I am somewhat disconcerted at this foretelling of shaky times ahead for me.

He also goes on about symmetry ranking high in the world of sexual selection and how depressing it must be to have a single mastectomy. Since I have had one, I am surprised at my lack of depression, although I must admit, that if I don't wear my prosthesis, I do tend to lean sharply to the left where I still have one rather large breast, and so am distinctly sexually unselectable, but at seventy-eight, who cares!

## ⅊⅃⅃ℵ

As an antidote to all Lawrence's musings on sex and Miller's on the perfectly symmetrical face, I picked up *A Shortcut Through Time: The Path to the Quantum Computer,* George Johnson's update on quantum computing. It is five years out of date, for one can only keep up with this kind of material by reading current journals. Still, I need an introduction to the subject, so I plough through every page of it. I absorb what I can by osmosis and let it float through my science-comprehension barrier as well as it can. Why, I wonder, wasn't I wired differently so that I could fully understand, say, what "a single-qubit rotation" might be? Still I am assured that nobody really understands the quantum view of the world even though it is used every day in various applications, so I don't feel too despondent. It's the same thing with gravity, I suppose, in that no one really understands gravity either, yet based on the assumption that it exists, endless practical things work very well. The odd time I have thought about how remarkable it is that I am standing upright while the earth is whizzing around, I get giddy and lie down clutching the rug for security, because the horrid thought that gravity might desert me personally has, for a dizzy moment, really penetrated.

I ask my son, Adam, a systems analyst, how I can better retain some of the simpler facts about quantum computers, or science in general, and he tells me that repetitive reading helps. I know that he is right, because as I read and reread, I am beginning to recognise many technical terms even though I would be hesitant to define them, if asked.

While still in the science world, in the book *On Being Certain: Believing You Are Right Even When You're Not,* I find Robert A. Burton, on the basis of his exploration of the latest neurological findings, declaring that our rational statements and firm opinions are decided at an involuntary level and we have little or no control over them. This fact should surely demand that we insert a "maybe" into all our dogmatic statements. It is a worrisome, even threatening, book because it shakes many of our beliefs, beliefs that we hold because we know they are right, or because science persuades us so. This book tells us that these beliefs are only probabilities produced from a filter layer of our being that predetermines, or weighs up ahead of time, any decision that we think we are making consciously. Burton declares that the heart of his book is this: "Despite how certainty feels, it is neither a conscious choice nor even a thought process. Certainty and similar states of 'knowing what we know' arise out of involuntary brain mechanisms that, like love or anger, function independently of reason." Is all religious experience a case of faulty wiring then? Is all creativity a lapse of synapses?

Seeking something familiar, or reassuring in Burton's troubling book, I come across Chuang-Tzu's wonderful request, "The fish trap exists because of the fish. Once you've gotten [sic] the fish, you can forget the trap. The rabbit snare exists because of the rabbit. Once you've gotten the rabbit, you can forget the snare. Words exist because of meaning. Once you've gotten the meaning, you can forget the words. Where can I find a man who has forgotten the words so that I can talk with him?" I love it, except who on earth was the translator who chose the unfortunate "gotten" so many times? What's wrong with "got"?

Because the brain can apparently "smooth out discrepancies by backward projection of the second image by as much as 120 milliseconds [Burton is speaking here of the difference between the processing of incoming sensory data and the moment of perception] 'being in the moment' is a virtual recipe that steals from both the recent past and the immediate future." So much for the "here and now" of haiku.

*On Being Certain* argues that the feeling of knowing something actually precedes our consideration of the idea, although it "feels" as though it comes afterwards. Oh dear. Burton advises that for deciding to choose small things such as a brand of shampoo one could deliberate, but that for big purchases like cars, it is better to do a stack of crosswords and let the unconscious do the weighing up of pros and cons. I've always believed that, even though I never knew why.

Burton concludes that our choice of science or religious belief merely reflects "stories we are telling ourselves about ourselves and the world we live in. Stated purpose is a personal hidden layer-based narrative – not a reasoned argument." His point of view is supported by John Searle, a contemporary philosopher, when he says, "Conscious states are caused by lower level neurobiological processes in the brain ... They have absolutely no life of their own, independent of the neurobiology." And Benjamin Libet adds, "Unconscious thoughts trigger our behaviour, our conscious explanations follow at a distance."

The thing about this book that is most upsetting for me is that Burton points out that some questions should never be asked. I suppose he means questions I frequently ask such as "What happened before the birth of the universe?" "Where does consciousness come from?" and "Why is there something rather than nothing?" This is because, as Kant puts it, "The physical mechanisms that shape the perceptions of our experience also shape the way we think about those phenomenon that we cannot directly experience." And yet biologically we can't help but continue asking these questions and seeking answers.

Samuel Johnson also realized Burton's theory of unconscious determination long ago when he stated, "All theory is against freedom of the will; all experience is for it." How could he be so perceptive?

Perhaps the last word on this matter should go to physics professor, David Gross, who says that "the most important product of knowledge is ignorance." There you go. I'll try and sort this all out later.

**ЛЛⳆ⃠**

Back to light summer reading and a swimmingly wonderful book it is too, for Roger Deakin, modelling himself on the swimmer in John Cheever's short story "The Swimmer," decides to swim across, around, and up and down the UK. His book is entitled *Waterlog*. His trip was a dramatic and exhausting cure for depression and it leaves the reader feeling both soaked and exhilarated. Deakin writes evocatively of both his passion for swimming and the history and legends attached to the rivers, canals, beaches, outdoor swimming pools, caves and mountain lakes he swims in. A perfectly beautiful book for swimmers and non-swimmers alike, it is an intimate sharing of both a natural element and himself. It turns out that this book sent the whole of the UK scurrying to look at its treatment of its waterways. I wish there had been a map in *Waterlog,* but as some of the swimming holes were secret and many were close to small villages, I suppose, as usual, I am asking the impossible.

Medieval quest, perpetual rebirthing, antidepressant, way of feeling more alive, searching the "genius of places" ... Deakin's swimming journeys were all of these. He quotes the once popular Frederick Leboyer from his *Birth Without Violence,* "The horror of being born is the intensity, the immensity of the experience, its variety, its suffocating richness... It is a sensory experience so huge, it is beyond our comprehension." Multiply that by the number of times Deakin plunged into water and you get the feel of this book. One small "out-of-body" description by Deakin is given when he is swimming in still water, "Mind and body go off somewhere together in unselfconscious bliss, and the lengths seem to swim themselves."

# ΛΙΔΙ\

By the way, John Cheever's much anthologized story, "The Swimmer," first appeared in the *New Yorker* magazine, which is not my favourite reading material. I live frugally on my small island, and while consumerism is not unknown on this island, it is mostly the all-the-clothes-you-can-stuff-in-a-plastic-bag-for-two-dollars at our GIRO recycling depot kind of consumerism. My daughter, whose close friend lives in Manhattan, is a frequent flyer to NY and loves the city. She sends me packages of old *New Yorkers* from time to time and recently, since I had just read an intriguing book by Janet Malcolm, a *New Yorker* staffer, I took the pile out of the cupboard where I had stashed them, and went through it looking for any article by her.

The book that I had just finished by Janet Malcolm was The Silent Woman, a book about the poets Sylvia Plath and Ted Hughes. In *The Silent Woman: Sylvia Plath and Ted Hughes,* under the guise of writing about Plath and Hughes, Malcolm actually wrote a book about the dangers of writing biography. She should know, since she was sued for ten million dollars by Jeffrey Masson for quoting derogatory statements that he said he had never made and that Janet had inserted in her book, *In The Freud Archives.*

A few pages into the book and I have completely lost interest in those self-absorbed poets and have become totally absorbed in Ms. Malcolm and her wonderful writing.

Here are some of her comments and sound advice on biography writing. There are many more in *The Silent*

*Woman,* but I just chose a few to show any of you who might be contemplating writing a biography, just how perilous the field is.

"The biographer at work, indeed, is like the professional burglar, breaking into a house, rifling through certain drawers that he has good reason to think contain the jewellery and the money, and triumphantly bearing his loot away ... There is no length he will not go to, and the more his book reflects his industry the more the reader believes that he is having an elevating literary experience, rather than simply listening to backstairs gossip and reading other people's mail."

"Relatives are the biographer's natural enemies; they are like the hostile tribes an explorer encounters and must ruthlessly subdue to claim his territory."

"The pose of fair-mindedness, the charade of even-handedness, the striking of an attitude of detachment can never be more than rhetorical ruses; if they were genuine, if the writer *actually* didn't care one way or the other how things came out, he would not bestir himself to represent them."

I must squeeze in a last quote which is again on biography. Malcolm comments that "what happens to historical accounts that don't add up is that they get rewritten so they do." And elsewhere still on the theme of biographers, they have "the arrogant desire to impose a narrative on the stray bits and pieces of life that wash up on the shores of biographical research."

Alright, I squeezed in two, but for future biographers can there ever be enough warnings? I'm sure everyone can name one or two biographies that they think are fine, but, for me, it would be hard to beat Juliet Barker's one-thousand-page, five-years-in-the-making *The Brontës*. It seems like an hour by hour record of probably the most famous literary family (the nine Waughs must be considered in the running also, since they produced one hundred and eight books in all!), and I read every word of it, their lives were so well told.

But back to *The Silent Woman,* for it too is wonderful writing and I make a note to check out what other books Janet Malcolm has written. As to Sylvia and Ted, why must poets be so unpleasant? Part of me wants to join the feminist hoards who call Ted a murderer (actually a double murderer, because the woman he left Sylvia Plath for also committed suicide and took their child with her), but the other part of me finds Sylvia histrionic, and wildly over-exaggerating her pain, e.g., she wrote a poem when she was fourteen years old, "I thought that I could not be hurt." The tragedy? Her grandmother had smudged one of her pastel drawings. Later she was condemned for comparing her father to Hitler and her life to folks that had been in Auschwitz. But then, again, as I mentioned earlier, suffering is relative and perhaps neither Sylvia nor Ted should be blamed for behaviour which might very well be accounted for by mental instability (on Sylvia's part) and too much testosterone on Ted's. Of course this raises the question – when can we be held accountable for behaviour possibly decided by our genes, the chemicals in our bodies or our conditioning?

Anne Stevenson, who had taken Ted's side in her book, *Bitter Fame: A Life of Sylvia Plath*, wrote "I believe Sylvia, encouraged perhaps by her Freudian and well-meaning therapist, Ruth Beutscher, found her own psychodrama (a word I prefer to "mythology") so intoxicating and such an inspiring source of poetry, that she lost all perspective."

Ms. Malcolm calls all the many articles and books on the pair the "Plath biographical enterprise." I wonder if Sylvia had not been married to Ted Hughes (later to be Britain's Poet Laureate) and had not committed suicide, whether her poetry would even be recalled today. I have heard opinions both ways; the jury is still out. Olwyn, Ted's sister, when commenting on Sylvia's poetry, asked, "Why doesn't she say something?" But then she would take that position, wouldn't she?

More on Janet Malcolm, the author of *The Silent Woman,* whose writing is very much engaging me at the moment. I just got *Two Lives: Gertrude and Alice,* her book on Gertrude Stein and Alice B. Toklas, out of the library. I have been very prejudiced against these two women, who cadged and wangled and collaborated in order to stay fed in comfort in France during the war, when fellow Jews were going by train to the camps. Because they knew the "right" people, they got extra ration cards, and none of their Picassos (which were left in Paris when they evacuated to the country) were touched. One terrible example of their stupidity and selfish insensitivity was the advice Stein gave to a group of young men about to be shipped off to

Germany, "learn their language and get to know their literature, think of yourselves as a tourist not as a prisoner."

On reading Janet Malcom's frank evaluation of them, I
am starting to wonder, however, if I wouldn't too have
sold out in order to survive; one never knows how one will
behave until one is tested.

Stein is rarely spoken of today and the only book I ever
read of hers, in fact the only book that was readable, was
the bestseller, *The Autobiography of Alice B. Toklas,* the
clever account of what is actually Stein's autobiography
written as if by Ms. Toklas. As Gertrude intimated, she
decided in this book to prostitute herself and write a book
in regular English that would be a bestseller. Still, by the
time I had finished Malcolm's book, I felt I could understand a little better that Stein was wrestling with words
like she wrestled with the enormous amount of food she
ate, chewing them over again and again to penetrate the
deepest flavour of meaning that she searched for in vain.
Her writing makes mine seem like tofu, something that
easily slips down the throat.

Malcolm describes Stein's writing style being "as if the
reader were an uninvited guest arriving on the wrong night
at a dark house." Delicious writing. Malcolm also comments,
"We never forget we are reading while reading *The Making of
the Americans* [one of Stein's 'impossible' books]."

## ⴼⵍⴰⵏ

It's the end of June and for some reason I'm feeling sad, so
a three-hundred-page book on prime numbers may be just

the answer to my woes. It is by Marcus du Sautoy and is called *Music of the Primes: Searching to Solve the Greatest Mystery in Mathematics.* As I read it I come across this nice distinction, "Some say that admitting the possibility of such a number ($\sqrt{-1}$) is what separates the mathematician from the rest." I wonder what separates the poet?

I don't mind getting library books with notes written in the margin. Marginalia is the official name for them. I like to picture a former reader of the book, with the book propped up at the table during a frugal meal at eventide, his brains more on the text than the meal. His wife is singing the children to sleep in the next room. Or perhaps vice versa. This thought was brought to mind by the copious comments and corrections that have been written in the margins of this library book on prime numbers.

The most famous note in the margin of any book was done by Fermat in Diophantus' *Arithmetica*. It read, "It is impossible for a cube to be the sum of two cubes, a fourth power to be the sum of two fourth powers, or in general for any number that is a power greater than the second to be the sum of two like powers. I have discovered a truly marvellous demonstration of this proposition that this margin is too narrow to contain."

Of course over the years many mathematicians have sought the proof that the "margin was too narrow to contain." At last in 1993 Andrew Wiles came through with a many page answer, and it also was much larger than any margin could hold. For this he got the Wolfskehl Prize.

Halfway through *Music of the Primes,* I find a challenge to factor a number into two primes. I am in an oddly good space by now and find myself writing down one hundred and twenty-seven as one of the factors of this six-digit number. I admit I thought about the seven since the number to be factored finished in nine, but the rest was automatic. Imagine my delight when I found it was one of the factors. I immediately wrote to Professor du Sautoy. A bottle of champagne had been offered for the solution when the book was first published, but it must have been claimed long ago. He replied to me, "I think solving maths problems is more satisfying than a bottle of champagne anyway." Eli and I also admired his book, *Symmetry: A Journey into the Patterns of Nature.*

To finish, a last quote from this beautifully written book, "'Immortality' may be a silly word, but probably a mathematician has the best chance of [attaining] whatever it may mean." Perhaps du Sautoy is basing his comment on G. H. Hardy's thought that "languages die and mathematical ideas do not."

## ⅢⳜⅠ\

I write continually of books and the writing process, but never of where to store one's ever-growing collection. As is my wont from time to time, I ordered a book by mistake, but in this case, it turns out that this is just the book you need if you are worrying about storage. It is called, *Living with Books,* so you can see how I easily made the mistake of thinking it was actually about the contents of books. This book has a multitude of photographs of bookshelves from the sublime (covering all walls) to the ridiculous (a coffee-table actually made of coffee-table books). Alan Powers, the author of the book, is the librarian of the Prince of Wales' Institute of Architecture. He is not much concerned with how your bookbindings match your wallpaper, but he does offer many practical, innovative and often beautiful ways to display and make readily available your most precious possessions – books.

The choice of books we buy to keep is definitely a reflection of ourselves, so giving a passing thought to the way we store and display them must also say something about us. This book offers you enough options to meet any idiosyncrasies you might have.

And "yes," I have finished *The Tale of Genji*. This colossal undertaking has removed any guilt I might have felt about discarding *Dr. Faustus* in January. In fact it has filled me with a certain hubris. Hubris is not good, but I know that in July I will be truly humbled by the quality of haiku produced by *haijin* coming to our annual meeting at our little vinyl-sided cottage, so I might as well enjoy the pride in my achievement while it lasts. I heard Royall Tyler on the radio speaking of his translation. He has the most beautiful bass voice, so I quickly check him out on Google to see what he looks like (I can be so trivial from time to time). He is rather good-looking, with a great smile and a fast-receding hairline, but far from my image of Genji. One can't have everything I suppose. Professor Tyler has been given one of the highest honours (the Order of the Rising Sun) that can be given to a foreigner by the Japanese Government, possibly for all his work promoting Japanese culture, but also, I suspect for this crowning translation of *Genji Monogatari*. I bask a little in reflected glory since I have managed to plough my furrow through it.

# July

This is my birthday month. For a summer baby, it is strange how much I dislike the heat. I cover myself with layers of thin cotton, don a floppy straw hat and stay that way until September. I look like something out of *Brideshead Revisited,* ready for croquet at the sound of a mallet.

**my birthday**
**I write a haiku for my twin**
**how can I forget?**

One of the advantages of being in your very late seventies is that people ignore you, so you can pretty well get away with what you want. Of course that's one of the disadvantages too. Why does life have to be such a paradox? Whatever my age, however, I always seem to feel somewhat older than I actually am as I work to deadlines several months away, and library readings booked for the following year, irrespective of whether I will still be around at that time or not. But then, who knows that piece of information?

I love meeting my readers, but I have only just realized that when I do read in public or speak on the radio, I always assume my audience is one of writers, or folks who aspire to write. I know that this is not correct, for some of my listeners will be caregivers and space scientists and bus drivers, but still I persist in this idea. So now I find myself wondering what these hypothetical writers do in between finishing one book, and commencing the next? What do they do when the poem they have written has shivered to completion, and another has not yet sparked on their page That is, how do they occupy the time between one creative act and the next?

For myself, I choose to read of other writers and their writing ways in these periods. I like to discover their ideas of what writing might be about, and of that mythical place where ideas come from. For this kind of reading, I can certainly recommend the three PEN anthologies of writers. PEN Canada helps (in whatever way it can) writers worldwide who are persecuted for the peaceful expression of their ideas. For over eighty years it has been lobbying governments and making the public aware when the freedom of expression is being challenged. As its Honorary Patron, John Ralston Saul explains, "PEN ... is about persistent interventions, letters, phone calls, pressure: all efforts in an endless campaign which writers can't afford to turn their backs on. For that matter, I don't think anyone can."

So feeling that I am supporting a good thing, and hoping that PEN will never have to come to my rescue, I have just finished the PEN anthology *Writing Life: Celebrated Canadian and International Authors on Writing and Life*. It contains fifty essays by well-known writers, most of them Canadian. One should not be intimidated by their biographies at the back of the book, which list endless awards that they have won. Rather, I take heart with the one author who declares firmly that he has won no awards.

Some of these writers' revelations I loved, some I disliked and one or two left me totally bewildered. Although I could understand every word on the pages, when these particular authors strung their words together, I had absolutely no idea what was being said. But then, I often feel that way when I read academic writing.

If you are around your late seventies, as I am, and your memory is slipping, the essays in *Writing Life* will blur together. I am no longer disturbed when I cannot remember who said what words of wisdom. I just let the fifty authors invade my psyche and tried to make sense of what I was left with at the end. Elizabeth Hay says it so beautifully when she describes such reading as "catching a ride on the coattails of literature." For whatever you come out with at the end, after entering the minds of fifty mostly interesting writers, one thing will be for sure that if you are like me, you will long to be part of all that angst and all that euphoria. Such books leave me searching around for a sharpener to get my pencil ready in order to put the words that are already spilling out of my mouth, down on paper.

Confusing the mass of comments and advice on life in general, and the writer's life in particular, my rather slippery memory quickly forgot who said what in *Writer's Life,* so I could no longer remember whether Margaret Atwood had had an epiphany as she looked down on Peterborough at night from a vantage point, or whether it was someone else. Was it Margaret Drabble who decided to give up on striving for perfection, for getting the concept directly reflected on the page, or was that Rohinton Mistry? Oh no, it couldn't have been him, because he contributed that witty piece – his address to the graduating class of 1999 at the University of Toronto.

I learned that other writers can be shy, can feel sick before a public reading, can have doubts about their talent, can love, and laugh, and cry buckets of tears. Yes, I learned that writers are very similar to non-writers only they are brave enough to put pen to paper and sit back and let "things happen in ways they had never foreseen." This last bit is a quote from Elizabeth Hay again, and that joy anyone can share.

How can anyone resist Marilyn Bowering's advice (I remembered this one), "Celebrities hire people to take care of it [she's talking about fame here]. The writer keeps writing books in the hopes that they will do. Silly writer. If you want to succeed in this game, if you really want to, better take your clothes off, or kill somebody, kill yourself." I really resonated with that advice, for a publisher (not my present one) had once indicated that he couldn't take me on unless I was willing to stand on my head and waggle my legs in public. I didn't go with that publishing house, but often wonder whether that is the reason I am always careful to wear fresh underwear nowadays when going to give a reading in public.

Constance Rooke, the editor of *Writing Life,* had an illustrious career as a literary critic and was a fervent champion of Canadian literature. She died in 2008.

Although she was a sophisticated academic, she was still able to ask a naive but interesting question in her introduction to this book. It was "why does the public expect writers to move towards fame, when they do not expect this of teachers, engineers or business men?" Reading these fifty writers doesn't provide an answer, but it will explain, to a certain extent, what drives them to write. *Writing Life* was a fundraiser for PEN. It is still available, and the purchase money still goes to that worthy cause. Susan Musgrave's essay alone is worth the price. I mentioned her thoughts on vulnerability earlier but here is the full quote. "People are always telling me, how it's dangerous to be so open and honest; I think my vulnerability is a disguise to cover my real vulnerability. The very fact of revelation is a way of hiding."

**Ⅱ⅃◢Ⅼ\**

I am much addicted to writers no longer in the limelight. For example, whatever happened to John Cheever, he of the *The Wapshot Chronicle?* I check our library and that book isn't even in the collection, so I settle for *The Wapshot Scandal.* All this activity because a friend had recommended Cheever's daughter's biography of him, *Home Before Dark: A Personal Memoir of John Cheever by his Daughter.* Like many writers, Cheever was an alcoholic. Alcoholism is a strange addiction to me. We rarely serve alcohol; it is not part of my social culture. I don't have to get drunk before I'm amusing, abusive, honest, etc., and from my childhood, one phrase I remember is *"schicker vi a* goy" (drunk as a non-Jew). There have certainly been times when, and places where, a Jew could not afford to get drunk in case there was a pogrom and he needed to have his wits about him. I do remember a bottle of eggnog, saved for my half-sister's wedding, exploding all over my mother's fur coat, but that's it as far as alcohol memories from my childhood go.

*Home Before Dark* is adequate and compelling enough that I finished it, but it is not inspiring. I'll wait a while before I tip my hat to yet another dead author who won all the prizes, hit the bestseller list and graced the cover of Time magazine once, and is now almost forgotten. I guess I must have mentioned to my friend who had recommended *Home Before Dark* that I had recently read *Waterlog,* the book inspired by Cheever's short story "The Swimmer," and that's what made her suggest the biography. At the time I was reading *Waterlog,* I'd ordered Cheever's complete short stories in order to reread "The Swimmer," and glancing in my book-box, I notice they've arrived. *Home Before Dark* has rather put me off Cheever, but being a person who likes a certain completeness in my reading, I decide to give his short stories a whirl.

After completing *The Stories of John Cheever,* I feel that I can now tell you anything you would like to know about the state of suburban married life in the years after the Second World War. Cheever says about them, "These stories seem at times to be stories of a long-lost world when the city of New York was still filled with a river light, when you heard the Benny Goodman quartet from a radio in the corner stationery store, and when almost everybody wore a hat." I find that odd because after reading *The Stories of John Cheever,* I am left with the distinct memory of a haze of unsatisfied suburban housewives and wandering academic husbands. Surely I couldn't have misread the stories so badly? My favourite story in the book turns out to be "The Swimmer," the tale about a man who swam home through suburban swimming pools. See, I was right, at least one story involved suburban life.

Cheever was the one who said, "I write to make sense of my life." He certainly gets points for that quote in my accounting book on writers.

Short fiction is not popular. I am not sure why, for short stories, like short poetry, are often intense and rich, as if the whole world has to be shown in a few pages. Still they are viewed as an author's stepchildren. Cheever was remarkably successful with that form, however, and so, of course, is Alice Munro, although some of her books of short stories, such as *The Beggar Maid,* have been viewed as a new form of novel.

A friend just lent me Munro's book *The View from Castle Rock.* It is a fictional memoir or autobiographical fiction depending on which part of the book you are reading. Just as Cheever moved from swimming pool to swimming pool in his famous story, Munro moves from generation to generation, the link being blood rather than water. When asked if the book was a series of memoirs, she replied that the stories "pay more attention to the truth of life than fiction usually does."

Munro has won so many awards for her short stories that her credits overflow the inside flap. For this book, however, the Giller Prize was not possible, for she was sitting on the Giller jury the year the book came out. The first part of the book, which tells of how her ancestors left the Scottish Borders to immigrate to North America, really resonated with me. I too had left the British Isles to come to Canada on an immigrant ship and can remember my feelings as the coastline of the homeland disappeared and later when landing in Quebec with no one to meet me. Even my much later small effort at organic farming on five Ontario acres, allowed me to mix with some familiarity with Munro's relatives' pioneering experiences. When she moves to recent years and her parents' attempt at fur farming, this pioneer spirit still pervades her stories. As she names her relatives, Munro muses, "Now all these names I have been recording are joined to the living people in my mind, and to the lost kitchens, the polished nickel trim on the commodious presiding black stoves, the sour wooden draining boards that never quite dried, the yellow light of the coal-oil lamps." These few well-chosen words of hers are enough to fling me back into my own pseudo-pioneering attempts in the seventies.

Her writing is beautiful and has that "clear seeing" of Alison Uttley in *The Country Child* and of Flora Thompson in *Lark Rise*. For example, about the farmers calling to their horses at spring ploughing time, she writes, "You couldn't hear the exact words, anymore than you could make out what the seagulls on their inland flights were saying, or follow the arguments of crows." Again, of a house servant, Munro says, "Every move she made had the energy and concentration of somebody rowing a boat against the current and every word she said was flung out as if into a high wind of opposition." So simple.

Her ancestors loom large in her memories. Mine, on the other hand, faded as sepia photographs, are too dim to be as compelling. Munro says of writing these memoirs, "We can't resist this rifling around in the past, sifting the untrustworthy evidence, linking stray names and questionable dates and anecdotes together, hanging onto the threads, insisting on being joined to dead people and therefore to life." Well, I can resist this, but I do terribly admire her rifling (or perhaps it should more exactly be riffling).

ᏵᏞ◢ᏆᏅ

I make a note to check my favourite second-hand bookstore in Nanaimo for some Munro titles. Gabriola Island's closest ferry-link on Vancouver Island is Nanaimo. On Nanaimo's main drag, there are three excellent second-hand bookstores. One, Literacy Nanaimo, has a volunteer staff and the money raised by selling donated books goes towards ... well, literacy efforts in Nanaimo.

I have a friend who volunteers there and I keep her supplied with an endless list of books to be on the lookout for, books which I seemingly need urgently. Books rank with food and shelter when it comes to my basic needs, so I was delighted to have an email from her telling me that a copy of *Love That Dog* by Sharon Creech had come in. *Love That Dog* is one of my favourite books, and I'm always giving it away, so never seem to have a copy on hand. The book has a good deal to do with something I am wrestling with at the moment – how to make poetry accessible.

The story tells how a young boy (who thought poetry reading and writing was just for girls) was converted because ... well, I don't want to be a plot spoiler, so I won't tell you how he got hooked on poetry (Oops!), but I will tell you that *Love That Dog* is about poetry that is both meaningful and interesting.

For me, writing poetry is a wonderful way to tell of things that I think need to be told, and in a very condensed way. If the way is too condensed, however, or cluttered with too many metaphors and too many idiosyncratic ways of saying things, the reader will not only be unable to find the truth in the poem, but they may well be turned off from ever opening another poetry book again. As Billy Collins, one of my very favourite poets, says, "I would suggest, 'accessible' would mean 'easy to enter,' like a building. An accessible poem has a clear entrance, a front door through which the reader may pass into the body of the poem."

I love the idea of a poem as a building, for after all, even the freest form verse still has a structure, otherwise it would be prose and not poetry. As far as accessibility goes, the reader can quickly see when they start a poem, and I quote Billy Collins again, whether "the building is either open or locked."

I like to be welcomed into a poem, myself. I don't have the energy to break and enter it, or the energy to decipher it as if it was some ancient code. It's not that I'm too lazy to use Google to search for some odd reference in the poem that I am not familiar with, nor that I don't require an element of mystery in a poem, for I do. It's just that I'm choosing to read poetry so that I can share an intense moment with the poet. A moment that I hope will change me a little and open me further to the human condition. I want the poem to help me in this, and so my plea is for it to be accessible.

If you feel the same way about poetry as I do, then start with Sharon Creech's *Love That Dog,* a book for kids that adults also love. I promise it will lead you to demand from your closest school librarian that poems from Billy Collins' two anthologies be read over high school PA systems every day after the sports practices announcements and news from the ecology club. The first anthology is called *Poetry 180: A turning back to poetry* and the second, for the first brought in thousands of enthusiastic letters from students across North America, is called *180 More: Extraordinary poems for every day.*

I like to read poetry where I know who is doing what to whom and so I try and write similar poetry myself. I am an everyday poet and write about petty everyday things in the hope that my readers will find that my poems lead them to view the everyday as pretty wonderful. Here is a poem I wrote the day after my birthday a couple of years ago. I had shared my party with a friend who had her birthday on the same day. Whilst getting her act together the next day in order to bring the remains of the cake over to my house, she rested the cake on the roof of her car. Rushing back and forth for other things to bring, she completely forgot about it and drove off at her usual speed. Needless to say, the cake never arrived. Here's the poem I wrote in its honour.

### Things that fall off car roofs

Things that fall off car roofs –
straw hats,
insulated coffee mugs,
laptops,
teachers' notes and
yesterday, the remains
of my birthday cake.
Today I stare closely
at tires on my small island,
looking for signs of sponge cake
lemon-curd filling
and fragments of chocolate icing
that once spelled
"Happy birthday, Naomi."

The poem is ostensibly about a small, very ordinary moment, but I realized, after I reread my first draft, that it is actually about the ephemeral nature of all things and the insubstantiality of the concept of time.

Yes, poetry can be about the everyday and still say as much, or almost as much, about the ways of the world as more ponderous works of prose. Try it for yourself and see if you don't agree.

ℿ◿⫙

At the same time as *Love That Dog* came from Literacy Nanaimo, I picked up a copy of D. H. Lawrence's *The Virgin and the Gypsy*; an easy book for a summer read, I told myself. Yet the reason for picking it up probably had noth-ing to do with summer and a lot more to do with the contrasting classes implied in the title – in this case the middle class and the outcast. I enjoy Lawrence's *Lady Chatterley's Lover,* because it also involves the mixing of classes. Although I doubt that I have any Anglo-Saxon blood in my veins, my English education certainly infused a class-consciousness into them; with class being defined by the way one spoke (we are talking of England seventy years ago here), the fashion labels on one's clothes and by the university one went to. I, even though brought up in a socially-conscious household, had a strange sense not only of class, but also of the empire and that we, England, owned all those red bits on the globe, and for that reason were superior in some way.

Lawrence, being from working-class origins, was terri-bly conscious of class and so these two books must have delighted him as a chance to strike a blow at the boring, dull, inhibited and pretentious English middle class. He himself categorized mankind into two classes: those with "born-free nature" and those with "base-born nature," and, of course, he identified himself with those that are born free, even though he was mother-ruled to a large extent.

*The Virgin and the Gypsy* is totally politically incorrect. It romanticizes the gypsies and barely gives one character a name, mostly describing her as "the little Jewess." I cringed every time I read the words. Still, he puts himself in the female mind as few male writers can, and when our heroine, the virgin, ponders at length on her hypocritical family and her growing attraction to the gypsy, I feel he has really hit target. Still there is a lot of "her will had parted from her limbs, he had power over her: his shadow was on her" kind of stuff about the melting virgin. And a lot of the gypsy being aware of "the mysterious fruit of her virginity, her perfect tenderness of body" and "the dark, tremulous, potent secret of her virginity."

What saves *The Virgin and the Gypsy* from being a Harlequin romance then? Perhaps it is Lawrence's ability to build up a sexual tension between the sexes; a will to overpower on the part of the male, and to be overpowered on the part of the female. All very evolutionarily natural, but totally anti-feminist. I remember the same slow buildup of tensions in *Lady Chatterley's Lover,* as the lovers slowly become aware of each other, without really knowing that their bodies have already made the decision. Somehow Lawrence does this so intelligently that the writing rises way above the average "true romance." I vow to make time to reread it. Lawrence, as summer reading, may not have been the best choice, for he is so earnest and serious, and his writing forces one to think about issues that are not made for balmy days at the beach.

**/IL⊿I\**

Even at the age of seventy-eight, twice a year I have a twinge of ambition, of hope, of desire for a new goal, perhaps a wish to be a little less cynical. This happens at New Year and also at the time of my birthday. Imagine my delight then when I came across a book on reading that is about being inspired by the authors one reads. It is by a college professor who takes a somewhat unorthodox approach to the teaching of the humanities by actually challenging his students and giving them space to see new possibilities, new directions and new aspirations for their young lives by asking them difficult questions and expecting them to find answers to these in their reading. The teacher himself is an inspiration. He is Mark Edmundson, a professor at the University of Virginia, and his book is simply called *Why Read?*

He points out that university brochures, in order to attract students, seem like a cross between Disney World and a luxury spa. The students are shown well-appointed dorms, phys. ed. facilities, and orchestra and drama troupes. Edmundson complains that the brochures are "retirement spreads for the young." Their accent is on enjoyment and ease and include no mention of challenge or failing grades. Apparently at U of V, professors themselves are graded in the first few weeks of term as students work out which courses they want to take. A teacher who gets known for giving Cs and Ds and asking students to think, to struggle a little, gets avoided, and so teachers modify to comply.

For his approach to teaching literature, Professor Edmundson uses Proust as his guide when Proust says that "it seems to me that they would not be 'my' readers but readers of their own selves, my book being merely a sort of magnifying glass ... it would be my book, but with it I would furnish them the means of reading what lay inside themselves."

Edmundson feels that questions such as who am I? What might I become? What is this world in which I find myself? How might it be changed for the better? should lie at the core of a liberal arts education. He points out that with TV, DVDs and the World Wide Web his students are addicted to watching and have become afraid of being directly confronted. Edmundson complains that they are capable of researching Dickens, but not writing as if they were Dickens.

Edmundson is a big fan of Richard Rorty, who makes a plea for people to learn "new languages," meaning new ways of seeing things, for both Edmundson and Rorty know that only when people have that capacity will they know that the beliefs, truths and commitments they hold today will always contain an element of doubt. Tomorrow they may be seeing and saying in better ways. Edmundson wants his students to be able to change their narratives and enlarge their "circles of self." Quoting Frost, Edmundson holds that "a truth ceases to be entirely true when it's uttered even for the second time."

And all this can be accomplished by serious literary study. So Edmundson hopes for flexibility in his students – that they will start his courses with a certain "sense of dislocation," a sense one "has lost one's way." Attention to written words, the "coaxing forth of disparate meanings" is important, but theory, Edmundson feels, "should not come between readers and literature." Critical reading should be in order to find visions that can be applied to the reader's life. The interpretation should not be judged as right or wrong, but "whether it leads us to a worldview that is potentially better than what we currently hold." The reader, the critic, should be "one who brings forth the philosophy of life latent in major works of art and imagination; he makes the author's implicit wisdom explicit."

Edmundson compares a first rapturous read as similar to falling in love, but he points out that to adapt the book's vision to one's own use, the lover has to go further and ask "what would it mean to live this vision?" He rightly points out that we all get conditioned by our upbringing, but that studying the humanities gives us a second chance. And that it is a teacher's job to help the student see what great books offer.

Well, you can see I'm all roiled up with this book, *Why Read?* by Professor Mark Edmundson, and with his vision of teaching. This roiling has yet to take form and get anchored to the ground. But getting roiled up in one's birthday month is about the best present one could receive.

**ᏕᏂ᎔**

I'm still basking in the feeling of a job well done with my completion of *The Tale of Genji* at the end of June. Eli and I decide to celebrate my birthday, *Genji* and the Heian Period (794–1185 CE) with sushi. This is not an entirely appropriate decision, for sushi did not appear in its modern form until the nineteenth century, but then when have I ever behaved entirely appropriately?

# August

It's blazing hot, the well is threatening to go dry and I'm definitely drying up on Lawrence. I've finished with him for the moment, having read *Women in Love, The Rainbow* and *The Virgin and the Gypsy,* and reread *Lady Chatterley's Lover* along with a couple of biographies. I'm Lawrenced out!

D. H. Lawrence was probably the most notable English writer of the first half of the twentieth century to come from the working class. How appropriate it is to be reading his books and about him on my island, the island that provided food for the coal miners of Nanaimo, since Lawrence himself came from a mining town and, indeed, his father thought that Lawrence might follow him down the pits. Yet, from what we know of Lawrence's mother, that was never going to happen. The biographies I read allowed me to soak myself in Lawrence. My choice way of getting to know a writer is to read as many of their books as I can lay my hands on at one period and also to read an autobiography, if there is one, and any biographies about the author.

Lawrence does go on about sex, doesn't he? And yet I don't find his books particularly erotic. He mentions all the correct anatomical parts with both medical terminology and their colloquial names, and takes us through seemingly endless passionate moments from the mildest "melting into each others arms ... afterwards they ..." kind to the caress-by-caress details of the whole engagement. And yet, it seems to me that though the animal passion might be present, he was not really writing about love, which is, of course, what I want to hear about. He tries to explain his intentions in his long introduction to *Lady Chatterley's Lover* when he says, "I want men and women to be able to *think* sex, fully, completely, honestly, and cleanly." One of the biographies I had picked up, John Worthen's *D. H. Lawrence: The Life of an Outsider,* does a brilliant analysis of his books with the emphasis on Lawrence's changing attitudes over the years towards sexuality. The shifts Professor Worthen indicates seem subtle to me and by the end of the book, I was totally confused as to whether Lawrence was seeking to shock his bourgeois audience, liberate sexuality from the closet, use it as a metaphor for class differences, or whether to interpret his writing from a Freudian mother-complex angle.

Whichever of these it might have been (probably all of them), the introduction of explicit sex caused his publishers a load of trouble, for bookstores and lending libraries would not carry them and, indeed, seemed to have strong powers of censorship in this respect. Curtis Brown, his agent, said, "If only he would turn out the great story which everyone expects of him, without any appearance or shadow of sex-obsession, he could have the world at his feet." Eight of his twelve novels received demands for cuts from printers, libraries and bookstores. In spite of all this, Professor Worthen considers Lawrence to be one of the least arousing, the least erotic of all sexual writers, and, although Professor Worthen did not provide his list of writers who write satisfactorily about sex, I think he may very well be correct.

For myself, the inadequacies of all the couplings in Lawrence's books, even when the couple do eventually get to the altar, seems to stem from his own basically unsatisfactory relationships. He had such a strong desire to be in control and this was pretty well impossible, for his strong mother had warped him, and his even stronger wife gave as good as she got. He puzzled in *Fantasia of the Unconscious,* "Man, the doer, the knower, the original in *being,* is he the lord of life? Or is the woman, the great Mother, who bore us from the womb of love, is she the supreme Goddess?" He never could make his mind up which image was truer. So, many of the relationships in his novels were those involving power plays as to who had the upper hand, who was the dominant God, as it were, or, I suppose one could say, who lay on top. Lawrence was not interested in women getting the vote or entering the work place. His idea of female liberation was that they should obtain erotic satisfaction. But even in this respect, it should not be at the expense of male potency.

The other biography that I read about Lawrence was an illustrated one by Keith Sagar, *The Life of D. H. Lawrence.* This book, with its numerous photographs, corrected the images I had created for myself of Lawrence and his entourage, and introduced Lawrence's basic dissatisfaction with himself, his chosen environment and the people around him. Lawrence seemed always poised for the next place to journey to. His restlessness makes for disturbing reading. What was he searching for? "Unknown, unworked lands where the salt has not lost its savour," he says. But more likely it seems he blamed the place he had temporarily settled in for his state of poor health, his lack of creativity, his foul temper, etc., etc. He could wipe out a whole area with a dismissal, such as his opinion that Sicilians, living in such close proximity to Etna, were "intellectual daimons," "intelligent and soul-less." Living near Etna, Lawrence said, "drove men mad." Dismissal with a large brush. Another time he attacks Spain through its wine, "my God, it is foul, cat-piss is champagne compared, this is the sulphureous urination of some aged horse ... and my malaria came back, and my teeth chattered like castanets – and that's the only truly Spanish thing I've done." No room for compromise there.

He was equally virulent with fellow writers dismissing Wells, Maugham and Walpole for the huge amounts of money they made, without a comment on their writing, and saying scathingly of Brett Young that "he has a great 'hall' in the Lake District, in which he can become a little more damp than he already is, to be a lake poet, instead of a mere puddle poet." Of Eric Gill he said, "Mr. Gill is not a born writer: he is crude and crass ... like a tiresome uneducated workman arguing in a pub." So much for identifying with the working man. I don't remember him having a word of praise for any other writer in all the many words I have read about him these last few weeks.

If it wasn't his fellow writers, then it was his friends that he was most critical of, and with Frieda, his wife, he was merciless. "Stick in your stomach, you bitch" was one of his milder commands to her. It caused me to self-consciously pull in my own muscles when I read it. Even though I have been known to be outspoken, I have never attacked my nearest and dearest as vituperatively as Lawrence dealt with his friends. It seems that he could never leave them alone when it came to pointing out what he perceived as faults. John Worthern comments that "writing and understanding were always more important to Lawrence than personal loyalty." An understatement if ever I've read one.

Frieda, his long-suffering wife, pronounced him a bully, although, as I mentioned earlier, she was certainly capable of retaliating in kind. What an odd couple! The worst bullying incident, often quoted, is when Lawrence kicked his dog, which was in heat and pulling in the neighbouring dogs; again rage at being unable to control the female, I suppose. Lawrence expounded the mastery that man must hold over women in *The Woman Who Rode Away,* and this brought down on himself the wrath of the feminist movement.

His works are riddled with his class-consciousness. On being rejected by the publisher Heinemann, and assuming it to be also a rejection by his middle-class readers, he wrote, "Curse the blasted, jelly-boned swines, the slimy, the belly-wriggling invertebrates, the miserable sodding rotters, the flaming sods, the snivelling, dribbling, dithering palsied pulse-less lot that make up England today." You can see he felt strongly about this.

Yet his insensitivity to those around him did not apply to landscapes, for he listed "acknowledgement of wonder" as one of three Native commandments when he lived in New Mexico. The other two being negative commands: "though shalt not lie" and "thou shalt not be a coward." He is speaking of the Aztecs here, and it may well, one suspects, be his interpretation, his selection from an unwritten code of behaviour. Having been brought up in a mining area, he deplored industrialization and all the evils that it brought to man's spirit and the environment. In the area of his own personal environment, his body, he avoided modern medicine and viewed his TB as "wounds to the soul." From my own experience, I now know that western medical advances should not be ignored, yet still something in me vibrates sympathetically with his view of the wound being to more than the flesh.

Seeking for some lightness in all Lawrence's earnestness, and as an unabashed quote-collector, I mark down Lawrence's take on the seated Buddha, "Oh I wish he would *stand up!"* I have actually myself, from time to time pondered how Buddha could possibly draw water and hew wood from the seated position. These practicalities do often concern me more than the abstract state of "enlightenment."

A possible last word on Lawrence (didn't I say that earlier? How he clings!). In his more humble moments he expressed his humanity this way, "feeling that one is not only a little individual living a little individual life, but that is in oneself the whole of mankind ... Not *me* – the little vain, personal D. H. Lawrence – but that unnameable me which is not vain, not personal, but strong and glad, and ultimately sure, but so blind, so groping, so tongue-tied, so staggering."

Whatever one feels, it is impossible to dismiss Lawrence as a minor writer. Somehow, throughout my reading of his works and of books about him, I have tried to sense what he was really yearning for, what he really aspired to. He seems to have had a hunger for a time that perhaps never existed, a time when people were involved in deep relationships with each other and with the world around them – its cycles and regularities – "the crisis of the winter solstice and the passion of Easter" as Lawrence put it. He searched for a kind of integrity within himself and with the environment surrounding him; a way where there was a balance between the mind and the body, between the soul and the body. A tall order that all his struggling, earnest words could barely describe and all his struggles with life could barely allow him to glimpse. In his story "The Man Who Loved Islands," he advised, "anyone who wants the world to be perfect must be careful not to have real likes or dislikes. A general goodwill is all you can afford." But like most of us, he didn't take his own advice.

### ⋔

It is still blazing hot, and now I am desperate to have a change from Lawrence's intensity. However, intensity is what I still get as I jump from the frying pan into the fire of Stephen Fry's enthusiasm. But this time it is Fry's joy of poetry that is so passionate, so I eagerly join him. Whoever would have thought a book on metre and form in poetry would be so much fun? This book is a brilliant three hundred and fifty page coverage of over two hundred and fifty poetry terms; everything from "acatalectic" to "zeugma." The name of the book is one of many terrible puns you will find throughout it, *The Ode Less Travelled: Unlocking the Poet Within.*

Apart from his tendency to scatological humour, which I find childish, Fry's asides are delicious and keep the pages turning through detailed analyses of stress and feet. For example, when speaking of lipograms, which are writings omitting a chosen letter, he comments wryly, "These days you might feel that a poem that never uses an 'I' would be a real achievement." And after a lengthy quote in Middle English, he comments that his spell-check had just resigned.

He really endears himself to me when, after giving a quote from the Ruba'iat of Omar Khayyam, he exclaims, "if that kind of poetry doesn't make your bosom heave then I fear we shall never be friends."

He complains, when speaking of a nonet, that "when people start to count, true verse dies." I feel somewhat the same about his pages of self-conscious iambs, trochees and spondees (no, I won't explain these, buy the book, it's worth every dime of its twenty dollars).

I wince when he informs (and I feel he has a direct line into my soul here) that "it's so much easier to say that everything you fail to understand is pretentious, than to learn to discriminate between the authentic and the fraudulent." He really attacked my Achilles heel, for I complain constantly about my inability to understand certain poetic forms, criticizing them, rather than reproaching my own inadequacies.

At a poetry reading I attended around the time I was reading Fry's book, a poet was talking about and reading concrete poetry. Eventually one of the many outspoken Gabriola folk demanded to know what the gobbledegook was all about. I'm ashamed to say I laughed out loud at her ability to say what others only thought.

However, having just finished Stephen Fry's love letter to poetry with form, I realise not all poets and all poetry readers are into the full variety of poetry forms that history offers us. Poetry that plays with words definitely goes against our Puritan culture, which demands that poetry should inform and communicate. Play seems to be a little outside of our understanding of what poetry's intent should be. Whether the poet literally plays with lipograms, acrostics and such writing, or whether he or she plays with words in order to philosophize about words and their connection to reality (in which case the purpose admittedly seems more solemn and acceptable) that poet is taking a risk.

It is a rare reader who can read sonnets, haiku, concrete poetry, cinquains and Hallmark cards with equal consideration. Even our lecturer on concrete poetry puts down Frost's poem of his trip through the woods, which I know is loved by many, and his interpretation of William Carlos Williams' "The Red Wheelbarrow" focusing on the number of words in the poem, is totally not mine, which focuses on the strong images. By the way I just love F. J.

Bergmann's response to this poem. It first appeared in the *North American Review.*

### An Apology
Forgive me
for backing over
and smashing
your red wheelbarrow.

It was raining
and the rear wiper
does not work on
my new plum-colored SUV.

I am also sorry
about the white
chickens.

*F. J. Bergmann*


Even if I love something to pieces, I am still detached enough to appreciate a little leg-pulling at its expense.

Our lecturer used examples of concrete poetry such as Jackson Mac Low's poem "The Presidents of the United States of America" in which the structure of images we are told is determined by the Phoenician (I stand corrected, but I think these are rather the Hebrew) meanings of the letters in the presidents' names. For example, in the section on Adams, "a" is represented by "aleph" (meaning the ox) so the poem would speak of oxen. Then the second letter of his name, "d" is represented by daleth (meaning door) so the word "door" would appear in the poem. Next "m" represented by mem (meaning water) would necessitate the mention of that word and finally for "s," shin (meaning teeth) would demand that the word "teeth" appear. You get the idea, I hope. Spontaneous poetry this is not. Perhaps "contrived" and "mind-controlled" would be too strong. Play it definitely is, the playing of an educated and interesting mind. Shall we call it poetry also?

All these meanderings stem from *The Ode Less Travelled.* Fry's fine book has been described as "an idiot's guide to the writing of poetry," but it is far from that, for his erudition and familiarity with all poetic forms draws you evangelically into the pleasure of reading and writing poetry. Even though it is a kind of textbook, I suppose, *The Ode Less Travelled* kept me accompanying it all the long journey. I even read the glossary at the end. It is not always this way with my reading.

**/IL⊿I\\**

Every time I open a new book, I do so with almost breath-less hope. Hope for what, I am not sure; but usually just after the middle of the book, my hope turns sour and I finish the book listlessly knowing that, yet once more, I have not found what I was seeking.

Occasionally, as in the Fry book, the book doesn't disappoint but holds its own until the last word. Another such book I have just finished by wetting the last page with a shower of tears. It is Michael Chabon's *The Final Solution: A Story of Detection;* a book that is a pastiche of a Sherlock Holmes mystery, but with a truly shattering ending. Not only did my attention not start to wilt halfway through, it held to the final full stop. The Conan Doyle style was perfectly imitated, but the denouement was extraordinary. What a truly original writer. I made a note to get his Pulitzer Prize winning book, *The Amazing Adventures of Kavalier & Clay,* also *Maps and Legends: Reading and Writing Along the Borderlands* and *The Yiddish Policemen's Union.* Don't bother asking why. Just go to the library and get Michael Chabon's *The Final Solution* and read it to the last line, particularly the last line. A slender volume that devastates.

By the way, I was charmed to know that a prizewinning story featuring Sherlock Holmes that Chabon wrote when he was ten years old made him decide to be a writer. He tells it this way, "I said to myself, 'That's it. That's what I want to do. I can do this.' And I never had any second thoughts or doubts."

For some reason my tiny island library responds faster than any big city one could, so I find myself spending a whole day reading about genres with which I have little familiarity – ghost stories, comic strips, apocalypse stories, science fiction. All this in Michael Chabon's book *Maps and Legends.* Are there really so many genres I know nothing whatsoever about? Still, this book contributed some profound quotes and I, as a collector of such quotes, was not disappointed with my harvest.

For example, when Chabon is speaking of his "God" of comic book writers and illustrators, Will Eisner, he quotes Flaubert, "An author in his book must be like God in the universe, present everywhere and visible nowhere." Does one need better advice as a writer? Chabon carries on this idea when writing of the golem, the mythical man produced from inanimate matter by adepts. He comments, "as the kabbalist is to God, so is a golem to all creation: a model, a miniature replica, a mirror – like the novel – of the world." As a word of warning here, Chabon quotes Gershon Scholem on the golem, "Like all major creation it endangers the life of the creator – the source of danger, however, is not the golem ... but the man himself."

The golem has long fascinated me, for the alchemical association of making life out of clay reflects the idea of God making Adam out of earth and also of artists, who create objects out of basic materials, for they too are in some way, "God written small." I can't remember who said this, but the ability to make something out of nothing, to make gold out of straw or lead – these were the legends of my childhood. I guess that's why I became a recycler of other folks' dross, so sure was I, and am still, that with enough energy, anything can be transmuted.

Chabon confesses that "anything good that I have written has, at some point during its composition, left me feeling uneasy and afraid. It has seemed, for a moment at least, to put me at risk." In this way he reflects the terror of the alchemist that his creation would overpower him. I would like to add that Chabon explains that the golem was built with the hope that it would bring the adept to life, as well as the golem. This too applies to artists and their creations.

Chabon comes to the conclusion about his own writing, "there was really only one investigation all along. One search, with a sole objective: a home, a world to call my own." Don't all writers seek to create their own reality? I know that I do.

Chabon's next book that turns up at my library is *The Amazing Adventures of Kavalier & Clay,* and it is truly amazing. *Kavalier & Clay* is a rich-textured, mature and totally wonderful book that held me completely, even though I have little interest in escape artists and almost none in comic books, the main topics around which the plot whirls. This is a great book and the fact it won the Pulitzer Prize didn't influence me in this opinion one bit. Coming across a childhood box of comic books reawakened Chabon's interest and resulted in this magnificent book. I wonder how many of us looking back to our early years can likewise see the seeds of our future endeavours?

I don't know why the following bit of advice from *Kavalier & Clay* stayed with me, but it did, "never worry about what you are escaping from. Reserve your anxieties for what you are escaping to."

Chabon seems to be breaking down some barriers with his writings, I think. Comic books, detective stories, horror stories, apocalypse tales and science fiction all seem to be treated by literary critics as second-class literature. Chabon looks to be demanding they be given an equal place. As Ruth Franklin put it, "Michael Chabon has spent considerable energy trying to drag the decaying corpse of genre fiction out of the shallow grave where writers of serious literature abandoned it." Lev Grossman expands on this when he states that "this [Chabon's writing] is literature in mid-transformation ... the highbrow and the lowbrow, once kept chastely separate, are now hooking up ... and you can almost see the future of litera-ture coming."

Considering Chabon's childhood influences reminds me that I have thought, from time to time, that I should have been a scientist. I mean an intuitive scientist, of course, not one that measures things and gets stuck in details. I suppose that is why I read so many books of science essays with such pleasure. And that is why I find myself asking "why am I scrubbing twenty straw table mats, some of them I haven't used in a dozen years, when I really want to talk about biology and literature?" Yes, biology and literature. Opera links literature to music, ballet links it to dance, but finding a book that links literary efforts to biology is a rarer thing. And it's not just any old biology that I am speaking of, but evolutionary biology, that cutting-edge science. The title, itself, would draw your hand towards it on any bookshelf – *Madame Bovary's Ovaries: A Darwinian Look at Literature*. It's all about evolu-tion, and clever David and Nanelle Barash, father and daughter, have taken some well-known novels and given them an evolutionary biologist's interpretation. Literature from the DNA point of view, as it were.

Male/male competition, female/female competition, female sexual selection, male sexual selection, philander-ing ... all the common plots of our beloved fiction are here explained from a survival point of view. Shakespeare's plays on the wars between the Lancasters and the Yorks become basically wars of genes. Philandering by the two sexes being "asymmetric" (that is, permissible in the case of the male, shocking in the case of the female) is clearly shown in many nineteenth-century novels, allowing Becky Sharp to be a notable exception, for she gets away with it, or does she?

The point the Barashes are making is that biology is not *the* key to understanding and appreciating literature, but that it is certainly *a* key. From Othello's jealousy to Huckleberry Finn and Holden Caulfield's rebellions, from Oedipus to Madame Bovary herself, the study of genes can certainly contribute to our understanding of the behaviour of our heroes, heroines and villains.

"Reading," the authors suggest, "makes more sense and is also more fun when informed by modern science's current knowledge of biology and of human nature." As someone who likes a heavy dose of science in my leisure-time reading, I nod my head in agreement. Let's heal the gap between science and the arts any way we can.

Fascinated by this very original linking of science and literature, I search Google for what else may have been written joining these two rarely married subjects. In my search, I come across a book written thirty years ago that fills the bill to some extent. *The Comedy of Survival: Literary Ecology and a Play Ethic* by Joseph W. Meeker explores literary works such as *Hamlet* and *The Divine Comedy* in order to discuss ecology and the state of the environment. It is a brilliant book that raises many serious questions and just goes to show that the latest top ten or Giller Prize winner may not hit the spot as well as a long-forgotten book. Bringing in an evolutionary element, Professor Meeker recommends comedy over tragedy as a survival mechanism, for comedy is of the commons. High ideals and poses lead to discord, disaster and death. Comedy keeps us moving through nonsense, surviving despite the fact that life is in all probability meaningless. If you've ever felt a need to justify a comedic approach to life (as I have from time to time) then this book is for you. It induced me to wax poetic.

### Restoring balance

A belly laugh returns everything
to normal, for at its sound,
the pompous extended stomach
bursts open, and tragedy moves
slightly off centre stage.
Romeo and Juliet, very much alive,
rush from the wings
and embrace at the footlights,
and foolish Heloise and Abelard
are prevented from ever meeting.
Heroics are shaved down to clowning,
and once more we shift around the stage
having children and muddling through.
With laughter, Death becomes
a cosmic sweeping-up of leaves,
and life a wonderment
of diversity.

/ΙↄΙΛ

I often wonder whether people have really read everything they say they have. Of course I have, and would never claim to have read say *Moby Dick* or Proust's *À La Recherche du Temps Perdu,* neither of which I will be likely to complete in the years I have remaining, though I may try

Thoreau's *Walden* for the umpteenth time because I feel it might have something to say about the zero-mile diet. By the way, Lawrence claimed that *Moby Dick* was "one of the strangest and most wonderful books in the world," and Ronald Wright declared that "if there has to be one great American novel, *The Whale,* is it." I am still not persuaded. All this non-reading brings me to the last book I will be considering this summer month.

"I never read a book I must review; it prejudices you so." Who else but Oscar Wilde could have said that, and it is the quote at the beginning of *How to Talk About Books You Haven't Read* by Pierre Bayard, which is the book of the moment for me. I am always a convert to the latest book I am reading. I speak constantly of it, if I like it enough, in the supermarket, at the library, when gossiping at Folklife Village of a Saturday and over the garden fence to my next-door neighbour who used to run a second-hand bookstore.

Before I tell you of this book, and in spite of knowing that I have half a year to go with my reading, I still hereby declare that this is, and is likely to be, the best book I have read this year. (Oops, did I say the same thing about *The Uses and Abuses of History*?) Under the witty and cynical examples of people speaking blatantly about books they haven't read (most taken from within books that we know the Pierre Bayard has read), Professor Bayard is really exploring reading itself and the role memory plays in the process.

Bayard, a French philosopher, makes his point using Sōseki Natsume's *I am a Cat,* Umberto Eco's *The Name of the Rose,* Musil's *The Man without Qualities,* Balzac's *Lost Illusions* and Greene's *The Third Man* (don't you remember clearly that wonderful scene when Martin gives a lecture knowing that the audience is expecting another author with the same surname and so has to talk to them about books he has neither read nor written), amongst many other books, in order to illustrate his point that you don't need to read books to be able to talk about them. Bayard points out that by choosing one book to read, you are eliminating the possibility of readings thousands of others and that it is really better to read books about books (what he calls "the collective library," the books on which our civilization depends) in that the true value is in understanding their interconnection. That's one up for me, thank you, professor.

Being culturally literate in this way, Bayard continues, one can get the feel of a book by barely reading it. "Who is the better reader," he asks, "the person who reads a work in depth without being able to situate it, or the person who enters no book in depth, but circulates through them all?"

Bayard quotes Paul Valéry about the reading process, "What I look for in a book is what will enable or impede an aspect of my own activity." We take a set of expectations· to a book so that no one is actually reading the same book with the same frame of mind. Again when we talk about books, "what we talk about is not the books themselves, but substitute objects we create for the occasion." These Bayard calls "screen books." Our memories of the books we read are selected by our needs at that time. Bayard also points out that since reading has to be accompanied by summarizing, it also involves forgetting, and so we are really, when we speak of the book we have just read to others, speaking of recollections, and again, none of us are discussing the same book.

Bayard expresses this all so beautifully when he says "that the path towards ourselves passes through books, but this must remain a passage. It is a *traversal of books* that a good reader engages in – a reader who knows that every book is a bearer of some part of himself and can give him access to it, if only he has the wisdom not to end his journey there."

Montaigne, my favourite essayist, quoted widely from his own reading, sometimes without attribution. He took what he needed from his reading in order to adjust his judgements, the name of the book and the author he had just read he usually managed to forget.

Bayard agrees with Montaigne in that we usually forget most of what we have read, and even when presented with a title can often say we haven't read the book, when we actually have. "If this is the case," he asks, "what is the difference between a book you have read and forgotten and a book that you have never read at all?" The answer to this might be perhaps only a small stirring of the psyche that went unnoticed at the time of reading.

Bayard adds to his concept of a collective library and a screen library, the idea of an "inner library," one filled with books that have left a deep impression on an individual. The "inner book" is what makes the screen book when the book is discussed. It is based on the set of myths (either collective or individual) that one brings to a reading, for this decides which elements of the text will be retained and which rejected.

Where inner libraries intersect, say during discussions in book clubs, the virtual library appears. This is an active collective library, as it were. And where screen books intersect, a phantom book appears; a book that was never written by any author, particularly the author we think we have just read.

I have a childhood memory of joining the eminent ranks of folks who talk about books they haven't read when I remember standing up in my English Literature class and earnestly telling the astonished teacher and my bewildered classmates, that I thought that Shakespeare was an anti-Semite. This at a time when I had only just heard of *The Merchant of Venice,* had not read it and barely knew what a Semite was anyway. I brought my own baggage to the play, and that held me back from ever entering any deeper by actually reading the play.

A last word of advice from Pierre Bayard on critiquing a book you haven't read, "Praise it without going into detail ... [The author] expects only that, while maintaining the greatest possible degree of ambiguity, you will tell him that you like what he wrote." I must say I do prefer upbeat fan mail, although I will take criticisms from a few people: my publisher, my husband (reluctantly) and, even a little harder to take, from my daughter.

Actually, I read *How to Talk About Books That You Haven't Read* twice and it is on my "frequently read" book-shelf, for I will doubtless read it again soon. Sorry, Pierre Bayard, I know I should have stuck to reading the back jacket, but this book about "not reading" is really about the urgent necessity of reading. My passion and Bayard's passion united in this totally wonderful text.

# September

Never say you've "made it" in life, for the moment you do, your neighbouring lot will be sold and logged, an old house will be barged onto it, a well will be drilled and your water will turn the colour of a slate roof! We had already had a week of well-digging across the road in June, but it didn't affect our water flow. However, this new well, next door to us, gives us an intimate connection with our new neighbour that we would prefer not to have. I had just bidden our last summer guest "Farewell," I had a pile of lovely reading in my book-box and the house looked as close to something out of *Better Homes and Gardens* as it's ever likely to get. I was beaming on the world when ... well, I really don't want to repeat the above, but to give you a clue, I haven't bathed in a week because our two bathtubs are full of water in order to be able to flush the toilets and the laundry is stacked behind the bathroom door because I won't wash it in slate-coloured water. After several temper tantrums, and after Eli has reminded me that my childhood "little princess" status hasn't applied for some years, I sulk on the deck to the accompaniment of the well-driller pounding away and try to think of searing, or at least wryly witty things I would like to say to those who have altered our lives so drastically in six days of ground-shattering thumping. As Nathan Englander writes in *The Ministry of Special Cases,* which has just entered my book-box, "troubles always start when they start for you."

Francine Prose's book, *Reading Like a Writer: A Guide for People Who Love Books and for Those Who Want to Write Them,* is just the kind of book I like to pick up to insulate me from the world at such times. Ms. Prose (what a suitable name) goes for the close-read school of teaching, where each paragraph, sentence and word the author wrote is explored in depth. A short story can take hours to go through with her class. While I appreciate the odd metaphor that spins me around with its brilliance, and the occasional use of the perfect word which leaves me gasping, on the whole, it is ideas I am looking for in books. It's those ideas, and hinted emotions, that allow me to take a long pause and consider life yet once more. However, I am always willing to take a deeper look at methods I find difficult, for the fault is usually mine.

I am horrified to think I have never analysed my reading as Ms. Prose has. I have never observed, as she does, when discussing questions in a text, "the shortest is a mere four words. The longest requires fifty-eight words, and a cascading succession of dependent clauses." My own personal reading seems to be done at top speed. Ms. Prose speaks of words, sentences, paragraphs, details that should be noted, whilst I read idly, awaiting the shiver I need before I know I'm reading genius. Only rarely do I chew a poem slowly. Often I wish I could be rereading one as I did the first time, with that first-time passion and excitement. As to the counting of words and dependant clauses, I just don't read that way. Maybe I should, at least once. She close reads to learn, I skim off the bits that help me find myself.

Well, Ms. Prose's book is fascinating and demanding, but David Sedaris' new book, *When You are Engulfed in Flames,* is sitting on the coffee table and it's raining for the third day running and ... well, I just feel like it, so I switch tracks and move from informed and informing to amused and amusing. I promise myself to return to the more demanding and definitely more essential-to-my-writing Ms. Prose later on.

David Sedaris must definitely be added, as perhaps my stepbrother, in the literary family I have planned for myself. He is a master at milking his family and has done so throughout all his books that I have read. Is he still really recalling incidents from his childhood, which seems to have stretched at least twice as long as the adult years he has existed, or are these just blatant lies and he has become a novelist?

Unfortunately, he just can't do it for me this time, for I'm still blue, although I've laughed out loud a couple of times during my reading of *When You are Engulfed in Flames,* his latest set of essays. His wit, however, can't make up for his foul-mouth, and his New York in-your-faceness is not the style here, several thousand miles away on my little island. He is still my choice for stepbrother when I re-family myself, but with certain reservations.

# /IL⊿I\

I'm back in balance, having finished knitting a great scarf of brown and white alpaca wool and having fingered through a few books of piano studies. I'm now, once again, seriously tucking into Francine Prose's excellent book, *Reading Like a Writer*, and remind myself that occasionally when writing (or reading come to that) I must pay more attention to the use of words, how sentences are formed and when a paragraph is declared finished. All these concerns she deals with in great academic style and I feel a little guilty that my own reading style is to speed along until, as I mentioned, I feel that rush of goose-pimpled arms that signifies the writer has hit the target, or at least my target.

Although one may be unable to read with Ms. Prose's intensity, I do feel that even the average reader, who maybe doesn't want to tear each sentence to pieces or dissect the book analytically, should still be aware of what they are bringing to a book – their conditioning, their prejudices, their closed or open minds – when they turn to the first page. They should also know what they expect from the book – escape, pleasure, to mine the riches for ideas, to find fresh goals, etc. Ms. Prose may not help you too much with this, for it depends on self-awareness, but she can still make you conscious of how much can be gained from a close reading of a book, even if that is not what you intend to do.

Ms. Prose defends reading in this analytical way by saying that the "stamina, concentration and patience" required will reward the reader, because they will be "approaching, as nearly as [they] can hope to come, the hand and mind of the artist." She demands the writer read, not in order to see what can be stolen or borrowed, but what can be "admired, absorbed and learned."

She knows that the writer needs enormous courage; courage to resist outside pressures to write in a certain way or "to follow a prescribed form," and courage to expose themselves to the world. Ms. Prose feels that literature is an endless source of courage and confirmation to the writer to do just that. Sometimes, as in Mr. Sedaris' case, perhaps courage is needed to not continually expose himself, and his nearest and dearest, but usually the courage is needed the other way.

Whilst speaking of courage, Ms. Prose includes "the courage not to give the work a happy ending." She gives as an example that marvellous ending of Chekhov's *The Lady with the Dog,* "And it seemed as though in a little while the solution would be found, and then a new and glorious life would begin; and it was clear to both of them that the end was still far off, and that what was to be most complicated and difficult for them was only just beginning." Why doesn't Cinderella have this coda?

Ms. Prose is passionate about books and asks, "Who can be saved by a terrific sonnet? Whom can we feed with a short story? The saving and feeding is not of the body, but we can at least save something." She doesn't specify what, but we nod in approval anyway in spite of not knowing either.

I envy Ms. Prose her reading style where nothing goes unnoticed, but I'm a skimmer. I can see myself getting a good job writing synopses, getting the gist and discarding the rest. And speaking of synopses, I do so love Woody Allen's synopsis of *War and Peace,* which he read supposedly during a speed-reading course. He defines it succinctly, "It is about Russia."

Having been filled with guilt that I had only read one third of the *1001 Books You Must Read Before You Die,* I am almost inured to others' lists. I fair badly on the booklist Ms. Prose recommends, having read only twenty percent of the titles. What have I been doing the last thirty years, I wonder.

**/ILⴠⵏ**

What is it with the end of summer and Judaism? We have now met three couples originating from Toronto, and not just from Toronto, but from the same synagogue in Toronto; and all gathered on our little island. I swear I expect their rabbi to turn up next summer. I tell them of Michael Chabon, they counter with Jonathan Safran Foer and with Nathan Englander – all bright young Jewish writers; sensations with their first books and handsome, powerfully handsome. Our hostess, at a dinner to celebrate the Toronto visitors, lends me Englander's *For the Relief of Unbearable Urges.* One of the Toronto guests tells me that he thinks "The Tumblers," one of the stories in it, is the best short story he has ever read.

The guest is a Cambridge Master of Arts. Never mind that Masters of Arts degrees are given automatically at Cambridge two years after you have your undergraduate degree, the fact that he reached Cambridge and that he graduated indicates some brilliance of mind, so I take note of his opinion. Although we arrive home late, I stay awake and finish the story. Yes, it is better than good ... it is breathtakingly good. I am curious as to whether it is the best story in the book, so the next morning I depart from my usual routine and finish the rest of the book. The stories are in Sholem Aleichem's style and take me to a part of Judaism that I do not understand.

Well, actually, I don't understand Judaism at all. I can't for the life of me understand why I should be considered Jewish just because my mother was. If she had been black and I also black I can see that there would be some connection with a racial group, but a religion? How can a religion be in my genes?

"The Tumblers" is superb. Most of the other stories in *For the Relief of Unbearable Urges* lack the sharp ending I always look for. Some peter away and some finish on a false note. I want integrity to the last word, and I'm not getting it always in this book. Still, that one story is worth all the rest bundled together, though it would be hard to say whether it, or any other, is the best I have ever read.

Most of all I wonder what someone reading it, someone with no knowledge of Judaism at all, and someone born long after the Holocaust, would think of the book, and particularly of that story. The man who recommended it likely can't step outside his skin to consider this possibility, but I can. It's a trick I've been able to do ever since I stepped out of the womb. The role of outsider, such as I am, while painful when one yearns to be ordinary like everyone else, brings some positives. One is that because one is not stuck in a particular point of view, one is able to adopt the best of the many interpretations of how life should be approached or what should be in one's moral backpack. One can explore all concepts, since one is not obliged to adopt any of them as one would be forced to if one belonged to a particular group. Buddha warmly recommended not getting stuck in concepts as a way to spiritual advancement, for any concept is only a partial view – particularly when seen from an outsider's position.

True to form, I try to read all the books by my current favourite, Nathan Englander. The only one that I can find reference to, besides *For the Relief of Unbearable Urges,* is his seven-years-in-the-writing novel, *The Ministry of Special Cases,* which is about Argentina's dirty war. That book had slipped into my book-box earlier in the month. It is about the powerful and the powerless and, when I read about this aspect of humanity, I identify with the defeated and the powerless, yet again. What a bloody world we live in. What is the point of it all? As usual, when I think an even slightly profound thought, I come up with a trivial one, this time it is that if I were to knuckle down to "serious" writing, I too might start and finish a novel within seven years. But could I speak of police corruption, anti-Semitism, government sleaze and dishonesty, brutality?

No, I could not, for my mind veers off when having to confront mankind's incredible flaws. It is as if I cannot conceive that human beings could behave that way; so, in my naivety, I push it to one side, knowing only too well that one day I will have to confront this aspect of humanity, if only within myself.

Kaddish, one of the figures in Englander's book asks, "How true is anything that only one man believes?" Elsewhere in the book his wife asks, "What I want to know from you is, if everyone believes the same lie, isn't it, maybe, the truth?" When will I stop puzzling such questions? Mr. Englander, elsewhere, in his essays, asks more questions, but these he sometimes at least partially answers himself, albeit rather disjointedly. "Is the Dirty War so large and ever present that one doesn't need to be reminded in order to remember? And then there is the more cosmic point, the message that the Mothers of the Plaza de Mayo send. And that is, events can be ignored and even actively forgotten, but it doesn't make it as if they weren't. History, if there is any such thing as truth, can't be undone."

It appears that Mr. Englander is now writing *Coward: a novel* and that it will be out sometime soon. I mark it as a book I must read, for this is a challenging young writer.

**/ﺎ\**

Having virtuously promised myself to read more slowly and with more consideration, after finishing Ms. Prose's book, and having tried to do this in Englander's *The*

*Ministry of Special Cases,* I turn to Harold Bloom's weighty tome *How to Read and Why.* The "Why" is in italics and I wonder why. It becomes immediately apparent that this book cannot be skimmed through, even if I want to, for Mr. Bloom's reasons for reading are scattered throughout the book and since I want to know them, I am condemned to reading his passionate analysis of books I will never read, such as *Moby Dick* and *À La Recherche du Temps Perdu.* I give Mr. Bloom points in that he has read every book he speaks of several times and in great depth. If only I wasn't contrary enough to feel that a haiku could sometimes, if it hits target, tell as much as any of the ponderous books he lists as great reading.

Where has he been the last fifty years that he chooses poetry, novels and plays from the past, with always Shakespeare as the benchmark? What about Rohinton Mistry, Wisława Szymborska, Michael Ondaatje ... the list is lengthy but even the few I've mentioned beat Hemingway and Henry James any day in my book. I prefer Billy Collins to Emily Dickinson – I find her dashes so distracting. A total aside but have you read Mr. Collins' wonderful poem called "Taking Off Emily Dickinson's Clothes"? It is one of my favourites, and no, I'm not a totally trivial person.

Never mind. I am going to race through this book and see how many of Bloom's reasons for reading I can gather together:

1) To thwart loneliness. (But what if the book disappoints, aren't we left just as lonely?)
2) To strengthen oneself.

3) Reading poetry can be a mode of transcendence, secular or spiritual, depending upon how you receive it.

4) Poetry is the only self-help that works.

5) To go home again (a bit cryptic).

6) To heal our pain.

7) If you read poetry aloud it gives you an enhanced sense of freedom.

8) To startle us out of our sleep-of-death into a more capacious sense of life.

9) To prepare us for change (he adds "and the final change alas is universal").

10) Bloom borrows from Francis Bacon and Samuel Johnson, and adds a touch of Emerson, when he advises, "Find what comes near to you that can be put to the use of weighing and considering, and that addresses you as though you share the one nature, free of time's tyranny." And he repeats, "Read deeply, not to believe, not to accept, not to contradict, but to learn to share in that one nature that writes and reads."

11) To strengthen the self and learn its authentic interests.

12) "The strongest, most authentic motive for deep reading of the so much-abused traditional canon is the search for a difficult pleasure." Yes, in the age of brief bites "a difficult pleasure" is a rarity.

13) "Turgenev's stories ... are as magnificent an answer to the question 'Why read?' as I know."

14) Quoting Henry Hazlitt, "Rereading old books is the highest form of literary pleasure, and instructs you in what is deepest in your own yearnings."

15) Cultivation of an individual consciousness (zest and insight are most enhanced by reading).

16) Bloom says that Proust "makes intimations that are too large for any social context whatsoever. These intimations reach out to the corners of our consciousness, and search for the principles of right action in us."

17) Because you can know, intimately, only a very few people, and perhaps you never know them at all. (Implying characters in books can be just as intimate as friends, I suppose.)

18) Only a deep constant reading fully establishes and augments an autonomous self. Until you become yourself, what benefit can you be to others?

But Mr. Bloom also warns or recommends us:

1) "It is not the function of reading to shore us up, or to console us prematurely."

2) "Do not attempt to convert your neighbor or your neighborhood by what or how you read." (Oops!)

3) "You need not fear that the freedom of your development as a reader is selfish, because if you become an authentic reader, then the response to your labors will confirm you as an illumination to others."

4) Quoting Emerson, "One must be an inventor to read well."

5) "The loss of irony is the death of reading" (though, as he points out, you can't teach someone to be ironic).

6) Quoting Wordsworth, "Read with wise passivity."

Oh dear! My prejudice is showing but I can't plod through pages of such comments as, "Borges' relativism is an absolute. Chekhov's is conditional." If you are used to this kind of analysis and know what he's talking about, Harold Bloom's book is for you. I've summarized all that he says on why we should read, and feel I have done my duty.

**ⅢⅬⅿⅠⅣ**

Although I rarely glance at a copy of *People* magazine or *HELLO!* at the Village Foods Supermarket checkout counter, I am not averse to literary gossip. So when I come across a mention in Bloom's book of Robert Graves' own sublimely destructive relationship with the American poet Laura Riding, Mr. Bloom has me off my chair and onto Google to see what that was all about. According to Louis Simpson, Graves had "come out of the Great War with shattered nerves and marriage to a woman he did not love. When Laura Riding appeared, he handed over the direction of his life and work to her – a dependence he would later come to regret." Well, if you have time and are still into intrigues, apparently you can read all about it in the book by Graves' nephew, Richard Perceval Graves, *Robert Graves: the Years with Laura, 1926-1940*. I don't have time at the moment, so their ménage à trios and ménage à quatre will have to wait for my old age. Graves' book, *The White Goddess: A Historical Grammar of Poetic Myth,* was certainly a revelation for many poets, including myself. I'm not sure knowledge of his sex life will improve my poetry, so will not pursue it.

Bloom catches me when he speaks at length about not minding poetry that needs a mediator (himself, I suppose). I, who would communicate directly with my own gods, resent someone having to carry the message of the writing to me. If I can't get what the writing means from the writing itself (giving it some of my modest skills at decodifying) I don't read it. I assume the writer wants to tell me something. If they do, then why do they hide it under layers of metaphors or obliqueness? No wonder academics, on retirement, go to writing workshops to re-educate themselves, so that they can write for the humble masses, instead of the privileged few. Ah, will I ever get rid of my Socialist roots? By the way, when Harold Bloom paraphrases Dr. Johnson's command to "clear your mind of academic cant" he is not speaking of the strange complexity of written communication by academics, but the demands of gender and sexuality and multiculturalism and other such areas where political correctness is expected (even if Dr. Johnson would never have used such recently-coined words).

I don't know if Mr. Bloom is trying to balance charges against him of anti-feminism (and worse), but he does go out of his way to alternate the he/she thing, in fact giving the word "she" far more presence than the word "he" in *How to Read and Why*.

I catch him on an error of fact. No, I'm not being petty, I'm just applying Ms. Prose's attention to detail. *Don Quixote* is not the first novel. The world's first novel was *The Tale of Genji* by Murasaki Shikibu, the book I triumphantly finished reading in June. While I'm at it with my trivia, did you know that *The Adventures of Tom Sawyer* was the first novel written on a typewriter?

Bloom is so adamant that there is no living female novelist to compare with Jane Austin or George Eliot and no poet to compare to Emily Dickinson and Elizabeth Bishop that I almost want to set several weeks of my life aside to consider this point and respond. As I'm dealing with dirty well water that threatens my two therapies for sadness – laundry and bathing – I can't spare the time, but quickly think of Doris Lessing off the top of my head.

I should learn from books that stir my guilt, but will I ever? This time the guilt is roused by my poor showing against Mr. Bloom's incredible sensitivity and passion for literature and poetry. His broad cultural reach allows him to draw aspects of writing together in their similarities and pull them apart in their differences. It allows him to make broad, sweeping statements such as "Dickens is not a Shakespearean novelist." It makes me regret my grammar-school education, which included only a little Latin, no Greek and by a long length not enough Shakespeare (that would be in Bloom's estimation). Still, I know a little about Japanese literature that doesn't seem to have hit Mr. Bloom's consciousness, so I shouldn't complain too much.

When it's not Shakespeare that Harold is pulling us back to, it is Marcel Proust. I have never met anyone who has completely read *À La Recherche du Temps Perdu,* and I doubt I ever will. Obsessive readers there are on Gabriola, but they are also tending their gardens and their firewood supply and their water-availability and other earthy matters that leave them little time to read of a few couples' erotic problems. There are enough of those too on Gabriola without searching more out in fiction.

One thing Harold Bloom has done for me though is to remind me that rhyme should not be totally banned from my poetry. When he quotes from *The Rime of the Ancient Mariner:*

> Day after day, day after day,
> We stuck, nor breath nor motion;
> As idle as a painted ship
> Upon a painted ocean

my heart still skips a beat, taking me back to my childhood and the resonance this image brought to a solitary child caught in family mayhem. Even today I love the slant rhyme (though I never use it), the rhyme that finishes a poem with a minor chord. Mr. Bloom quotes:

> The moon's my constant mistress
> And the lovely owl my marrow;
> The flaming drake and the night crow make
> Me music to my sorrow.
>             *(Anonymous, "Tom O' Bedlam's Song")*

I suppose the slant-rhyme "marrow," "sorrow" is counter-acted by the "drake" "make" in the third line.

Well, considering I rarely dip into most of the books Harold Bloom recommends, I must have been much struck with his discourse, because I finished up by reading every word of *How to Read and Why* and it has nudged me to places I was reluctant to visit, and stirred me out of a certain complacency, and that is why reading is good for you.

Harold Bloom's book was as tough going as Stephen Fry's, and although I am unlikely to follow Fry's path of formal poetry or Bloom's path of classical reading, yet I have learned that people take other reading (and writing) paths than my own, and that it is alright. I have also learned a little of why they do so. We are still linked by our love of books, though the ones we choose to read or write may vary widely.

## ⅡⅬⅬ\

My husband and I take, on an average, twenty books between us out of the library each Saturday. He keeps his in an old fruit box on the window seat beside his dining room chair. I keep mine in my book-box (actually an old milk crate) next to the couch and my afghan. My pile has dwindled and I don't fancy reading any of them today. I wander over to Eli's pile, and flipping through the books on evolution, economics and the brain that he has selected, I find slipped behind a large book the small book of short stories by Borges, *The Book of Sand*. To me, Borges is a writer of the imagination. He writes of infinities and libraries with books without end and books with pages without end and countries where they worship one word. This word turns out to be "wonder" though, sticking to my guns, I'm sure it was really "maybe." Borges' references are erudite and exotic and his stories leave you dangling in midair, or lost in a labyrinth without a clue of how to get out. He speaks to you across a café table, yet his words (though you understand each separately) muddle your mind into confusion and frustration.

He wrote, he said, for himself and his friends and to "ease the passing of time." It is the latter, I think, that might be his main reason, for it is infinities that he is drawn to, and when you are dealing with infinities, time melts into an abstraction, an abstraction that torments.

Many of his characters are blind, or almost so, and of his own blindness he says, "gradual blindness is not a tragedy. It's like a slow summer dusk." I resonate with the Platonic theory he allows someone in one of the stories to expound, "we have already seen everything ... so that to know is to know again." He then adds Bacon's comment that "if to learn is to remember, not to know is in fact to have forgotten." Delicious stuff.

"The Library of Babel" is not in this collection. In it, Borges supposes a "crimson hexagram," which is a book that is a log of all the other books in the infinity of books in the narrator's library. "A librarian who reads this log, is akin to God," so says Borges. This seems to me to echo the "collective library" of Bayard, in which knowing the interconnection of books is more important than reading each one.

Although I am not nationalist enough to seek the Canadian content in any and every event I come across, Borges does have a Canadian connection that is quite fascinating, for the young Alberto Manguel became reader to the blind Borges. In his teens, Alberto Manguel was a bookstore clerk in Buenos Aires. Borges enlisted Manguel to read out loud to him. Manguel was employed for several years (beginning in 1964) to go to Borges' apartment and read books chosen by the author. It is reported that when Borges composed poetry, he would dictate line by line (including the punctuation) to Manguel, who would write it down. You can read all about it in Manguel's 2006 book, *With Borges*. Alberto Manguel has probably read more widely than almost anyone else now alive. *The Globe and Mail* says "among English speakers, perhaps only Harold Bloom, George Steiner and Guy Davenport may outclass him – and they are all twenty years his senior, and long-time university teachers, to boot: In short, Manguel's approach to books remains resolutely that of an amateur, one who loves with the pure joy sometimes denied the more scholarly." He certainly is one person whose reading habits I aspire to, although there is little chance I will even approach.

# October

The languor of a dry summer is completely past and I am now alert and ready to tackle a couple of science books. I picked up another book by George Johnson, since I had enjoyed his *The Ten Most Beautiful Experiments* so much. In that book, Mr. Johnson, who is an excellent science writer, pointed out that these days it takes teams of scientists to make a breakthrough. When the top quark was discovered, for example, there were four hundred and thirty-nine names on the paper. In *The Ten Most Beautiful Experiments,* Mr. Johnson celebrates experiments done by one person or, at the most, one and an assistant; experiments that changed the way the world viewed that particular area of science. We have Harvey's discovery of the route our blood takes and Lavoisier's analysis of the constituents of air. From Galileo to Robert Millikan, Johnson takes us so intimately into the labs of scientists that we could almost be doing the experiments ourselves. This is a rare talent. Although there are other good science writers around, George Johnson gets my vote for making experiments real and beautiful and, most of all, understandable.

This second book of his that I turned to is *Miss Leavitt's Stars: The Untold Story of the Woman Who Discovered How to Measure the Universe.* The subtitle is not exactly true. Well, part of the book concerns the little that is known

about Miss Leavitt, but most of the book is about cosmo-
logical theory and that part is clear and fascinating. But it
is Miss Leavitt that I wanted to hear about. I had been
thinking of writing a book about women in science, uncel-
ebrated women, women whose supervisors got the Nobel
Prize, while they stayed back in the labs doing the grunt
work. Women such as Rosalind Franklin, who worked on
the X-Ray diffraction images of DNA, which Watson and
Crick were given access to without her knowledge, and
Jocelyn Bell Burnell, who found the first known pulsar.
They both missed the Nobel Prize that they maybe should
have received. In all fairness, Rosalind Franklin was dead
when Watson, Wilkins and Crick got the prize, and therefore she couldn't have been included. Nor would she have
been had she lived, because Maurice Wilkins, although her
peer, was the one named, along with Watson and Crick,
and not more than three people can be granted any one
Nobel Prize. And while I am talking about unrecognized
women in science, I should mention that Harlow Shapley,
Miss Leavitt's boss, got an entire cluster of galaxies named
after him, whereas Miss Leavitt was honoured by just one
crater on the moon receiving her name.

Perhaps it's just another example of Miss Leavitt being
taken advantage of in that the title, which implies she will
be featured large, doesn't really reflect the book's
contents. I've found a number of misleading titles like that
recently. I do understand how the title sells the book and
therefore must be catchy, but as the last half of a book
often lets me down anyway, I dislike having the title do
this also. One of the recent mismatched titles that I came

across was Daniel Coleman's *In Bed with the Word* and that title might have fooled you too. I'm not sure what I was expecting, but I know it wasn't the following explanation. It turns out the title is taken from an incident when a young boy, away at boarding school for the first time and very homesick, puts on his pyjamas and returns to bed with a copy of the Bible and, when asked by the matron why he was doing this, he responds, "I just thought I'd spend the day in bed with the word."

This book will also teach me to check subtitles, for this one reads *Reading, Spirituality, and Cultural Politics.* The word "spirituality" always makes me groan, but since the book is about reading, and reading is what I'm exploring these days, I proceed with caution.

It turns out to be a splendid book. I ignore all references to God about whom I know nothing, and, I suspect, when it comes down to it, nobody knows much more. What I am left with is a pleasant and well-reasoned discourse on reading with focus, intensity and passion. Even the word "spirituality" is treated in a way that I can meet halfway, for Daniel Coleman defines the word as "something that clearly flows through our religious impulses and experiences, but it is not identical with them, for it also flows through our psychology and physical sensibility, as well as through our social and political lives." I'm still a bit lost, but when he adds, "by spirituality, I mean a drive, or energy in ourselves that is outward-reaching, that is a kind of longing to be meaningfully connected," I feel we are making some contact with each other. He tops this with, "I mean what finally moves us, what propels our actions and sparks our imaginations, I mean a recognition of ourselves as connected to others, to the surrounding world ..." Well, why didn't he say so in the first place! The fact he finishes the sentence "and – within or beyond the sensory world – to the Creator," I ignore, for who knows how the world began and what might have existed before its beginning, taking us back into an endless spiral search for the initial cause ... which itself needs an initial cause.

I've just remembered that I have been guilty of mismatching title and content myself when I wrote an introduction to the Japanese language and called it *Japanese – an appetizer.* I thought this title was appropriate because it was just an hors d'oeuvre, as it were. However numerous indignant buyers thought it was a cookbook and were amazed to find the book a language how-to. *Zen and the Art of Motorcycle Maintenance* comes to mind as another deceptive title. As the author, Robert M. Pirsig, himself confessed, "It should in no way be associated with that great body of factual information relating to orthodox Zen Buddhist practice. It's not very factual on motorcycles, either." I'm sure you have your own list of mismatches.

ﾊﾑﾍ

I have just whizzed through a book that had been in my summer-read pile that I hadn't got to. It had been recommended to me as a quick, pleasant read. After all that science I thought I would take a light break, and so dipped into *The Guernsey Literary and Potato Peel Pie Society* by

Mary Ann Shaffer and Annie Barrows. The book seems to have had endless praise, one reviewer even describing it as "reminiscent of Helene Hanff's *84 Charing Cross Road.*" I had high hopes for it since the book had everything: wit, romance, tragedy ... what else could one ask for? It seems I am hard to satisfy though, because *The Guernsey Literary and Potato Peel Pie Society* just didn't work for me. The book is partially about the occupation of Guernsey by the Germans and, having recently read *Suite Française* about the occupation of France, the pie society just didn't nourish. It was "telling about" whereas *Suite Française*'s author knew the reality of what she was speaking. I don't want you to think I can't read something light for pleasure, but in the book (the title is too long for me to write out continually), each character seems carefully chosen, as if in a country-house-weekend detective story. There's one mean, uptight lady; one ingenue; a sad hero; a wonderful child. I know stories have to have characters, but in this case they have been so carefully chosen and the Guernsey wartime research is so obviously worked into the tale, that it all feels a bit too contrived. Though the book has been compared with one of my all-time favourite books, *84 Charing Cross Road,* for me the pie society came up lacking. For me it was lacking edge, it substituted reported tragedy for real tragedy, and textbook romance for the real thing. I wanted to like *The Guernsey Literary and Potato Peel Pie Society* so much because I respected the people who recommended it to me. Perhaps I'm taking it too seriously after reading of Miss Leavitt and the cosmos, or perhaps, as usual, I'm asking too much. I did, however, get one lovely quote from it that really resonated with me. It was made by one of the members of the Pie Society who only read one book, and that continually, *The Letters of Seneca*. He says, "I think you read more if you're laughing at the same time."

# ɅʌɅIɅ

Of all the hundreds of books that pass through our house in a year (most of them from the library) occasionally I will jot a title down and send it over to a couple of second-hand bookshops that I frequent, for I desire to make its impermanent borrowing into a permanent possessing. Two recent jottings have been *Lavengro* by George Borrow and *Ethel & Ernest: A True Story* by Raymond Briggs, and they have just arrived.

*Lavengro* is a book I only knew one quote from, but that a perfect one. I know that I already mentioned it in February, but I'd like to repeat it again for you here. "There's night and day, brother, both sweet things; sun, moon and stars, brother, all sweet things; there's likewise a wind on the heath. Life is very sweet, brother; who would wish to die?" According to Borrow, "lavengro" means master of the word, and the word in this case is the Romany language.

*Lavengro* was well worth waiting for because the narrator, while not a Romany, wanders with them and learns their ways and language. He has the strange purity about him that I continually look for in my characters. George Borrow knew many languages as an amateur and did, in fact, behave very much as his hero in the book, so that it is hard to know what is fiction and what is autobiography.

# ΛLΔΙΝ

Briggs' graphic novel, *Ethel & Ernest,* the second book that had arrived, covers a period in the UK that in my own life starts with when I was still living in England and ends many years after that, when I had departed for Canada. It is the true story of Briggs' parents' lives as retold in pictorial form by Mr. Briggs. It is warm, loving and heartbreaking. Could one ask for more? Briggs is, of course, the teller and illustrator of those two children's classics T*he Snowman and Father Christmas.*

If you're not familiar with graphic novels, I should say that graphic does not mean explicit but graphic in the sense that it is an illustrated book. Nor are graphic novels necessarily novels. The term "graphic novel" has come to describe serious content in comic book form, and distinguish it from the usual comic book content.

Other graphic novels that I wish I still had in the house are the set of three books covering the Hiroshima years, *Barefoot Gen* by Keiji Nakazawa, and one that covers the Holocaust, Art Spiegelman's *Maus.* These two books cover two of what must be the most terrible events of the twentieth century: the bombing of Hiroshima in 1945, and the Holocaust and the death camps that were set up to remove Jews, gypsies and other fringe people who didn't qualify for Aryan designation.

We carried the former book in our catalogue when my husband and I had our educational book business, Pacific-Rim Publishers, and got into loads of trouble with sensitive teachers because of its clear representation of what it was like to be a victim of the atomic bomb. The peeling skin and burned-to-a-crisp bodies were just too much for tender students apparently; students who frequently spent whole days playing at shooting and killing on their video games.

*Maus* is a remarkable tale of the death camps because the protagonist in this true story, the illustrator's father, is a singularly unpleasant person, and so we are not presented with good and bad but with persecutor and persecuted. At what age should a child be presented with these two graphic novels, which present two great tragedies of the twentieth century, the Hiroshima bombing and the Holocaust? The answer seems to hang in the air somewhere, but still the question demands a response.

Thinking of these graphic novels brings up memories of manga (Japanese comic books) from the time I lived in Japan. Manga are extremely popular and every salaryman and housewife would have one open on the train to pass the time. I often peered over their shoulders to see if I could follow what was going on. The manga ranged from soaps to pornography. I would immediately take my eyes away when the latter was being perused by some staid gentleman in pinstripes, though I sometimes glanced back, as I left the train, to take a look at his face and wonder what kind of a husband and father he was.

# ΛΔΙ\

My daughter-in-law, Sonhi, is Korean. Knowing of my interest in things Japanese, she once advised me to read Japanese history from a Korean viewpoint. I had never found the right book, but recently a book was recommended to me on Japanese culture. It was written by a Korean, and I can now see what Sonhi meant. The book is *The Compact Culture: The Japanese Tradition of "Smaller Is Better,"* and the author, O-Young Lee, was at one time South Korea's Minister of Culture. Canada has the Minister of Canadian Heritage and Official Languages, but that just doesn't quite seem to hit the spot as well as the clearly defined South Korean position. At any rate, Professor O-Young Lee is cultured, erudite on Japanese culture and wonderfully original. He is not vicious when dealing with Japan's treatment of Koreans, but points out, where necessary, the wrongs that were done to Koreans who had been taken to Japan during the Japanese occupation of Korea.

His thesis is simple: Japan does "small things" best. When they switch from reduction to expansionism the results are horrific. "Their sense of subtlety disappears, their capacity for judgement is impaired, and their natural susceptibility to beauty turns to brutality." As Korea has usually been the first target of Japanese expansionism, Professor Lee knows whereof he speaks.

The book is mostly about the paring away of non-necessities that makes traditional Japanese culture so spare and exquisite. He gives examples of folding fans (where the two-dimensional flat Chinese fan becomes a one-dimensional line); haiku (where the whole universe is trapped in seventeen syllables); *kokeshi* and Daruma dolls (where arms and legs vanish and the face becomes the essence); the Japanese flag (perhaps the simplest in the world); shrine gates (*torii*, consisting of just two uprights and a bar across the top); *kana* (the writing syllabary simplified from the complex borrowed Chinese kanji); and even the speech, where so many words are merely the first word of an implied phrase, e.g., *dōmo*, which means (depending on circumstances) "thank you," "sorry," "hello," "goodbye," "how very ... kind, or sad, or fortunate, etc."

Professor Lee illustrates Japanese excellence in the art of reduction by exploring not only poetry, but such cultural skills as *Nōh* drama, *ikebana* (flower arranging), bonsai (miniature trees) and *bonseki* (landscape in a tray). It is not only by "taking away" that Japan has shown its greatest strengths, but also by concentration: time stopped in the moment of a haiku, the frozen poses of the kabuki actors implying so much, Hokusai's *The Great Wave Off Kanagawa* capturing all giant waves that have ever formed. Also the back of things are important in Japanese culture – the sensuality of the nape of a woman's neck as the kimono collar stands away and the *obi* (kimono belt) elaborately tied at the back.

Japan pulls things towards it. The diminutive gardens of bonseki and the miniature trees of bonsai pull landscapes into the home. Instead of going to the mountains, the Japanese recreate them in their rock gardens. The picture postcards that we send home from our travels, the Japanese recreate on small screens, on fans and in their backyards. The marsh's edge and the mountain meadow are copied in the flower arrangement in the *tokonoma* (an alcove reserved for the display of scrolls and ikebana).

The very gods themselves are pulled into the house as Buddha sits in the family *butsudan* (Buddhist shrine), and the Shinto gods perch on the *kamidana* (the shrine shelf). The infinite is reduced to manageable and concentrated forms.

Professor Lee cites a wonderful example of this pulling of the world into Japan rather than going out to build empires in a haiku by Issa, where the poet tells of seeing the Milky Way through a small slit in his paper windows. Again, in a poem by Ishikawa Takuboku, the poet speaks of the Eastern Sea, then of an island within it, then of a beach on the island and finally of a small crab on that beach, thus reducing the boundless sea to something that can be intimately described – a small crab.

Professor Lee starts *The Compact Culture* with a quote from one of my favourite Heian writers, Sei Shōnagon, "All things small, no matter what they are, all things small are beautiful." He finishes the book by speaking of Japan's miraculous economic expansion of the '80s, and makes a plea by stating, "When they have moved out into the world, with the sword or the abacus, it has only been for themselves. I hope they will try again, but this time with world peace and mutual understanding as their goal." The book is dated, having been written at the peak of Japanese economic expansionism, but the theory still holds well.

# /ILⴍⵏ\

Having just seen the DVD, *Japan's Longest Day*, about the day the emperor decided to make the speech that meant the end of hostilities, I muse for a while on the evils of expansionism and empire and of all the havoc it has caused. This reminds me that I have just finished another book on one of the historical results of expansionism – slavery. In new colonies, when native populations died from imported diseases, or were killed off, workers had to be brought in to be servants, to work in the fields and the mines of the conquering Spanish, Portuguese, Dutch, French, Belgians and British. Slavery was not unknown in the Americas before this time, but empire building certainly swelled the number of people brought over to the colonies and enslaved there.

The book is *The Book of Negroes* by Lawrence Hill. Margaret MacMillan, in what will definitely be one of my favourite books of the year, *The Uses and Abuses of History*, gives many examples of history being slanted towards a whitewash of the recorder's actions. In Lawrence Hill's book, one certainly gets a new impression of Canada's part in the mistreatment of Africans dragged to the Americas. All we usually hear of is the Underground Railroad secreting slaves from the US South to freedom in Canada, whereas *The Book of Negroes* clearly records North America's first race riot as being in Birchtown, Nova Scotia, when unemployed white gangs attacked Black Loyalists' homes. The Black Loyalists had had their names written down in a recording book called "The Book of Negroes" before they left New York, bound for freedom and promised land in Nova Scotia. What they got was little better than the poverty and slavery they had come from.

The story in *The Book of Negroes* traces a woman from her African village, where she was captured, enslaved and taken to America. Later, disappointed in the promised move to Nova Scotia, she agrees to return to Africa and the shaky 'free' settlement at Freetown, Sierra Leone. It is a terrible story, a story of human greed and inhumanity and Mr. Hill spares us nothing. As one character says, "Child, evil ain't got no roof." Yet at the end, the comparatively happy end, the story (for me at least) seems to lack the edge of say Rohinton Mistry's *A Fine Balance*. I can't quite put my finger on it. *The Book of Negroes* is history written large and a compelling read, yet it didn't fill me with the gut-wrenching kind of despair that *A Fine Balance* had.

Oddly enough, what did bring me to tears was Lawrence Hill's thanks to his wife in the acknowledgements for the fact that, "She told me she loved me every day of every year that I gave to the novel, and fed and cared for the children and me while I pounded away on the keyboard." The tears, which should have come from the tragic story, came to me from this image which was intimate and closer to home, I guess.

**ᴨᴧᴉᴎ**

Although I go on about the work our property necessitates as if I was in servitude myself, after reading *The Book of*

*Negroes,* I swear I will never complain again. At the moment, I am merely fretting about the many chores I have to do before I put the garden to bed for the year. Just the thought of them makes me a little weary. As you will have noted from my April entries, I often prefer reading about gardening to actually doing it, so while making my garden to-do list, I began to once more think about garden writing and folks who do it.

Michael Pollan points out so nicely that writing and gardening are both ways of rendering the world in rows. His garden rows, reminiscent of his grandfather's, are straight, but his writing is circuitous. His wonderful essays in his books (*Second Nature: A Gardener's Education* being my favourite) wind this way and that, with each winding revealing a fresh point of view on a mundane gardening aspect. He described his own garden to his ninety-year-old grandfather in a touching way, "It was one of those places that is neither exactly in the past nor in the future, but that anyone who gardens is ever moving toward." One of my favourite bits of his writing, also in *Second Nature,* questions Thoreau (as I often do). To Thoreau's queries, "Do [these beans] not grow for woodchucks too? ... How, then, can our harvest fail? Shall I not rejoice also at the abundance of the weeds whose seeds are the granary of birds?" Pollan succinctly replies, "Sure, Henry, rejoice. And starve." Now that's my kind of garden writer.

If there is one book all recent garden writers are agreed on as a fine example of garden writing it would be Eleanor Perényi's *Green Thoughts: A Writer in the Garden.* Her name suggests an Edwardian lady with a touch of the

Hungarian exotic. Her picture on the back of this book is of a dyed-blond with a cocktail glass in one hand and a cigarette in the other to remind you that her opinionated and witty comments come from a one-time managing editor of *Mademoiselle* magazine. Take fifty garden topics, gather reference books, dig up garden gossip of past and present, add what your own hands and eyes (and other senses) have taught you and weave it all together into enchanting small essays and you will have done what Eleanor Perényi did when she wrote her one, and unfortunately only, gardening book. The chapters are dense and worth chewing over carefully. Her opinions are forceful, and even though they may be incorrect, at least they don't waver. In regard to Jerusalem artichokes she comments, "... even the flowers are inferior. Away with it, I say!" It would take a strong soul to try growing Jerusalem artichokes after reading that, I would imagine. Des Kennedy quotes and denies her firm affirmation that "two companionable people, who have assembled their material, can prepare an asparagus bed in a long springtime afternoon ..." But then Des and his wife garden on a pile of rocks in the Georgia Strait, so what can they expect. When speaking of asters, Ms. Perényi says, "I can't resist them and invariably let optimism get the better of judgement, which come to think of it may be the first principle of gardening." When writing of a garden full of the newest and showiest hybrids, she compares it to a woman with a facelift. Delicious writing.

Des Kennedy himself is high on my list of garden writers partly because he covers my neck of the woods, living, as he does, on Denman Island, which is close to Gabriola Island. His writing is also full of delightful metaphors, is rarely didactic (although he knows his subject well) and is never boring. He makes me laugh out loud and that is always a plus, since most garden writing fills me with feelings of guilt and insufficiency. I can forgive him going over the top occasionally in his writings, as he does when he compares our relationship to trees to Inuit throat singers as they exchange breath back and forth. His description of a storm on his shallow-soil island could describe a storm on Gabriola: "lying awake during a storm, rigid with terror, I wait for one of the giants to come down and flatten our house. Anyone can add this kind of excitement to their lives by simply getting a huge, shallow-planted tree growing close to the house on the windward side." Close-to-my-home writing and wonderfully accurate. And who but Des would have a chapter on money in a gardening book, as he does in *Crazy About Gardening: Humorous Reflections on the Sweet Seductions of a Garden*. Here he points out the dangers of the two extremes, "Too much of it [money] can overwhelm a garden as sure as too little may impoverish it ... The insolence of wealth leaches charm out of a garden as surely as incessant rain leaches out nutrients."

Other gardening titles worth a whiff: *French Dirt: The Story of a Garden in the South of France* by Richard Goodman (a charming story of a short-lived garden near Avignon); then there's the amazing story of the flower business, *Flower Confidential: The Good, the Bad, and the Beautiful* by Amy Stewart (everything from sexual harassment in the Ecuadorian greenhouses to Dutch flower auctions and high-end New York florists – a modest bunch of tulips and roses at seventy-five dollars!); another book by Michael Pollan, *The Botany of Desire: A Plant's-Eye View of the World* (his brilliant essays on four plants – apple, tulip, marijuana and potato); and the garden classic of someone considered by aficionados in his time as possibly the best garden writer alive, Christopher Lloyd. Although he is now dead, his book, *The Well-Tempered Garden,* lives on. Someone please bind and gag me, there are so many great gardening books out there.

Whether garden writers should be active gardeners seems weighted towards the dirt-under-the-fingernails school of thought. Paula Panich's claim that "writing about gardens and plants has been placed firmly into a cultural category, at least in this country [USA], of something that smells faintly of genteel ladies' cologne and has the feel of flower-trimmed hats worn to luncheon" is firmly counteracted by smart, tough garden writing in books such as Jamaica Kincaid's *My Garden (Book)* offers. What's for sure, as Des Kennedy points out, "writing and gardening are very similar callings. Once you've got the itch to do either, nothing this side of the apocalypse can stop you."

When I write about my garden, I restrict myself to poetry, for as Ms. Kincaid quotes Isidorus (she's not sure whether he is the one from Miletus or the Bishop of Seville), "If one does not know the names, one's knowledge of things is useless." As I don't know the names of many things in the garden, or have forgotten them even if I once knew them, my experience of the garden is mostly moments; the moment when everything clicks into place and the world sings, and for such moments, haiku are demanded.

sudden wealth
open forsythia and crocus
on our breakfast table

Gardening is an artificial thing, a man-against-nature kind of activity where, over time, nature usually manages to cover things with vines. Still, as Michael Pollan states hopefully, "The garden suggests there might be a place where we can meet nature halfway," and on some days when the roses are in full bloom and the fruit is ripening on the loaded trees, one can almost go along with those hopes.

# November

Already Santa costumes are being taken out from the mothballs and thoughts are turning to buy, buy, buy. Well others' thoughts may be, but definitely not mine, for I rarely shop for anything but basic staples. I lead a simple life, so I am a little surprised at myself for having spent the whole day reading *Deluxe: How Luxury Lost Its Luster*, a book by Dana Thomas about the luxury clothes business and the mad world of women whose hobby is shopping! Excellence I can understand – good quality material and fine workmanship – but buying dresses at twenty thousand dollars a garment, and shorts with ragged edges and simulated patches for two hundred and fifty dollars can only be examples of poor moral choice. Louis Vuitton handbags are marked up thirteen times the cost, I'm told. How can that be justified in a world in which so many are overwhelmed with poverty? When I was in the publishing business I was advised that a modest mark up of five times the cost was usual, but then that is an industry where businesses open and close almost as fast as restaurants.

Of course, it is easy for me to be judgemental, after having learned to live in style, way below the poverty line, as I have done in various parts of the globe for the last thirty years, and now being settled on a small island with few luxurious temptations. Yet I am not beyond temptation. Years ago, I wrote a poem about the designer Vionnet, whose miraculous garments both attracted and repelled me.

### Pin tucks
I look at the lattice
of pin tucks that
Vionnet has created;
coming down from
the left side
and the right side
and interweaving between
the stomach and groin
in a mystery of tiny stitches.
And, knowing this garment
is for snagging a rich man,
and knowing the gap
between a woman
who could buy such a dress
and a woman covered in rags
snatched from a barrio heap
will spell the death
of my planet ...
yet still I wonder
at Vionnet's cunning
and the skill of
the seamstress ... and
what it might feel
to one day wear
such a miracle myself.

Over-consumption has become morally repugnant to me. If each time we shopped we took the whole world's welfare into consideration, we would certainly choose to consume less. But then, that's just one more impossible thing I'm asking of the world. Shopping does not even cure personal depression, although many people behave as though it will. My mother would buy a hat when she felt depressed, and the hat boxes piled up in the cupboard, while she lay in her darkened room every afternoon.

I overcome my own moments of sadness by writing a poem, knitting a scarf or planning a new workshop. The last option forces me to seize what talent I have, and turn it outwards to encourage others. I find encouragement and cooperation to be sure cures for mild depression. Still, sadness is just the other side of the happiness coin and perhaps we should allow ourselves to sink into sadness a little, without getting totally lost, in order to see that laughter and tears seem to be the dual necessity of this three-dimensional world.

Consumerism, as *Deluxe* describes it in the world of fashion, seems personified by Sarah Jessica Parker in *Sex in the City* – of this series I seem to recall only a continual stream of shots of her character, Carrie Bradshaw, encumbered with designer carrier-bags emerging from exclusive clothes shops and wearing teeteringly impossible shoes. Goodness knows she had plenty of tears in her onscreen life that hardly seemed compensated for by her incredible outfits.

/ll◿ll\

Thinking of the upcoming holidays and their demands, causes me to feel out of sorts and have low energy, so I lie on the couch and cover myself with my security blanket, and pick up Sonja Arntzen's translation of *The Kagero Diary: A Woman's Autobiographical Text from Tenth-Century*

*Japan.* I love such days when I can read from an interesting book and let my mind drift, for that is when ideas come up for poems. To be more accurate, it is more that my mind, rather than drifting, actually whizzes around like a prayer wheel, snatching phrases that inspire, and transmuting them into haiku, or tanka, or the occasional full-blown essay.

Sonja says of her translation, "the text is disjunctive in the sense that the narrative is constantly being interrupted by poems, the quotations of voices of others and the intrusion of the author's own thoughts as bits of interior conversation." Hmm. That sounds a lot like the way I write, only I hope I don't whine as much as the writer of the *Kagero Diary.* She doesn't seem to have her own name, as is common in characters in the writing of this period, merely being known as Michitsuna's mother, so maybe she has good reason to complain. As Sonja Arntzen says in her powerful introduction to the book, "the diary could have well been subtitled 'I married the prince and we didn't live happily ever after.'" Whiny, or not, the *Kagero Diary* is a fine book and really filled the spot, perhaps by just allowing me to feel once again positive about my own reasonable life and my own reasonable prince charming.

Estelle Jelinek notes that women's autobiographies through the ages are "episodic and anecdotal, non-chronological and disjunctive." What a nice word "disjunctive" is. I have never seen it used before, and here, on one day, I have seen it in print twice, once from Ms. Jelinek and once from Professor Arntzen.

# ⫼⧄⫾

*The Book of Negroes* was suffused with suffering and suffering seems to pervade the next book I pick up too. It is *Cloud Atlas* by David Mitchell. This very ambitious book, a finalist for the Man Booker Prize, appears to be "among the most-honored works of fiction in recent history" according to Wikipedia. It is, indeed, a daunting work, consisting of six stories, each one being sufficient to fill a book in itself. The stories break off rather sharply halfway through and then, at the centre of the book, it is as if a mirror appears and the stories get their endings, each in turn, in the last half. As a reader of senior years, the fact that I have to abruptly change moods six times as a totally new story begins after the previous one has been left cliffhanging, and then, having read those first six halves, I have to try to remember where the stories left off, as I pick up and read their six completions, is testing, to say the least.

The stories are vaguely linked by, for example, a diary in one story being discovered by a character in the next, or a manuscript of a story being sent to a character in another. There is also a mysterious birthmark that appears in most stories. Mitchell explains the book by saying that "all of the [leading] characters except one are reincarnations of the same soul." The "cloud" in the title apparently represents the constantly changing appearance of what is really fixed, "the atlas" of human nature.

There is a lot of cleverness in this book that goes way over my head, for some of the science fiction episodes reflect a genre I am not familiar with; and the futuristic episodes emulate Orwell and Atwood, the latter of whose dystopias I also have not sampled. My favourite episode is "Letters from Zedelghem," in which a young and rascally composer writes a *Cloud Atlas Sextet,* again picking up the idea of a six part division of a creative work. I learned elsewhere that the young composer was based on the real-life Eric Fenby. The famous composer that he cuckolded in *Cloud Atlas* was a rather fictionalized Frederick Delius. As is my wont when reading literary gossip, I googled "Fenby" and no matter where I read, there was no hint of wicked behaviour in his relationship with Delius. In fact, he had not only to act as amanuensis to the blind and dying composer, but also as his nurse. Plus he had to put up with Delius' tantrums.

*Cloud Atlas* seems a very Darwinian book to me, as races threaten to disappear and sole survivors fight for a new way of life. The fragility of it all brings up my usual feelings when I have enjoyed a book, and these are that life is really too bitter to endure, and yet far too sweet to give up.

**ɅɅ**

Google, that helped me with Fenby, I must admit has become as necessary as footnotes, or annotations in margins for me – I am rather dependant on it for searching out facts, or clarifying points that I desperately need to know and which the author that I am reading at that moment has failed to provide. How many people annotate the books they read, I wonder. I can't remember who said that marginalia was "the reader's engagement with a book." I suppose one can be engaged without covering the pages with one's pencilled thoughts, but I find the definition attractive.

Readers seem to fall into two categories, at least librarians might divide them so, those who write in the margins of the books they are reading, and those who would never dream of doing so. Librarians are of one mind only – "Don't do it." That is, unless the same librarians have a chance of acquiring a book whose marginalia were entered by some famous person, or, even better, by some noted writer adding second thoughts to their already published manuscript. We're not speaking here of students' notes to a high-school textbook, we're talking about Samuel Taylor Coleridge (who introduced the word "marginalia" in 1819), or Edgar Allan Poe. I can't remember who told me this, but I have been informed that students buying second-hand textbooks will actually look for those heavily laden with margin writing, letting the previous owner do some of the heavy thinking for them.

The definition of marginalia varies widely, but it usually includes all drawings, doodles and editorial comments by readers. Those intended (and printed in the published book) are also called marginalia, such as the supplying of background information to the text as Martin Gardner did in his *Annotated Alice,* in which he annotates Lewis Carroll's *Alice in Wonderland* and *Through the Looking Glass.* Fiction books contain much less marginalia than non-fiction, I suppose because the kind of mindset that is present when one reads fiction differs from the more questioning mindset that non-fiction often demands. Marginalia implies, to me, that the reader feels they know something the author didn't, or that the reader feels their opinion is superior to what is in the book in some way. That may be another reason why fiction receives less marginalia.

Marginalia are a kind of one-sided conversation or argument with the author of the book (John Hollander describes it as shouting at the dead), since the author can offer no immediate response. A later response is possible, however, as in the case of Cyril Connolly who once saw a copy of one of his books in which Evelyn Waugh had entered very negative comments. His delayed response was to sell off a number of first edition, autographed copies of Waugh's books that he owned.

One-sided margin conversations can often be one-worded as one frequently sees, "Wow!" "Whatever" and "Read!" Anne Fadiman says that marginalia makes the monologue into a dialogue. But the first response to the written word has to be the last then, for the author cannot jump from the page and respond. I feel the writer of marginalia is actually altering the text, even if it's only with praise, and thus later readers of the annotated book have to deal with two books, the book they chose to read and the book with marginalia that they are presented with.

I sit on the fence when it comes to writing my own marginalia, using hasti-notes on relevant pages and a gentle mark in pencil at the phrase or passage I want noted. After I have finished the book, I enter the marked sections into a file, and then, gently but meticulously, rub out any sign of pencil. Were I to enter the marked passages directly into my machine as I read them, I think my reading absorption might get broken. I do think writing marginalia (even if it is just a line to indicate the entrancing passage) keeps me more alert and involved with the text.

My husband, Eli, is very careful where he writes in books. He usually makes notes of all the errata (and believe me there is never a book without an error some-where in it) on the inside back cover, and, if he has really enjoyed the book, will send a list of them to the author. A few have replied gratefully. One, however, wrote to their webmaster (their website being where Eli had found a gross error), but the email got returned to Eli by mistake. After telling of the correction needed, it commented, "Someone with time on their hands!"

Writing in your books does, in some way, establish your ownership of the book, making a firm statement that the book is yours and you can do what you want with it. Heather J. Jackson calls this BEPU (Book Enhanced for Personal Use). Ms. Jackson has actually written a whole book on marginalia, *Marginalia: Readers Writing in Books,* and while academic, it is most intriguing and readable. Who would have thought so much could be written on the subject. I like her position that if A stands for the annota-tor, and the person against marginalia is B (for bibliophile), then B thinks A stands for "anarchist" and A thinks B stands for "bore."

Montaigne, my favourite writer for so many reasons, told how he would often pick up what he thought was a new book only to find it full of his very own marginalia.

This is reassuring to older folk, such as myself, who can be twenty pages into a book before it rings a bell that some-time in the past they have read this book before. David Pryde expounds on note-taking in this way, "For how can you be intelligent [readers] without being discriminating; and how can you be discriminating without distinguishing between the good and the bad, the remarkable and the commonplace; and how can you distinguish between these without affixing some distinctive marks!" Well, yes, David, but does it have to be on the printed page?

Billy Collins has a marvellous poem on the subject (it is actually called "Marginalia") and it just about covers every-thing that needs to be said on the topic. The poem finishes by telling of some greasy smears that he found on a page and beside it in soft pencil, "Pardon the egg salad stains, but I'm in love." Even the most hardened librarian couldn't resist that one, could they?

And while we are on the topic of love, one of my students recommended *Last Lovers* as the love story to yearn for. I didn't find it so. It is the tale of a middle-aged man and a woman in her seventies who is blind, and how they accidentally meet in Paris (supposed to be the most romantic of cities, although I doubt that includes the suburbs). Their growing in-depth relationship is interest-ingly, although rather excessively anatomically, described for my taste, and I should really have cried buckets at the ending, but I merely found the hero's behaviour somewhat criminal and wondered how he was going to handle it, should there have been a next chapter. Oh dear! Am I becoming even more cynical in my old age? The writing is strangely innocent and naive and I look up the author, William Wharton, on Google to find that he is quite well-known and a late bloomer, like myself, having written his first book, *Birdy,* at the age of fifty. I'm told that the relationship between an older woman and a very much younger man is considered chic these days, so I eye my fourteen-years-younger husband with a little more attention after reading *Last Lovers,* having taken him for granted for over thirty years. The book may well have changed my outlook a little. I wonder whether he will notice.

## /IL⃠I\

Some love stories have achieved the rank of a cult book. For example, Erich Segal's book, actually called *Love Story* (the film was a precursor), became the number one best-selling book in 1970.

Cult fiction, to an extent, could be considered the marginalia of fiction, not that they are asides to the mainstream, for some of them, as *Love Story,* are bestsellers, but that their subjects are usually those on the fringe, on the outside. These books are often quirky, if not kinky, when they are compared to the usual run-of-the-mill books. *Love Story* is an exception in this respect, although apparently qualifying in others.

I've just gathered three books on the topic, since I feel this is an area I am ill-informed on and so wish to know a little more about it. I should start by telling you that, as a reader, I come off rather badly in the lists of cult books that the three books provide, having read only one in six of two of the book lists, and one in three of the book whose list is most moderate in its selection.

The books are *Cult Fiction: A Reader's Guide* by Andrew Calcutt and Richard Shephard, *The Rough Guide to Cult Fiction* by a large variety of contributors, and the most academic of them, *Classic Cult Fiction: A Companion to Popular Cult Literature* by Thomas Reed Whissen. The first, by Calcutt and Shephard, compares cult fiction to rock and roll in that just as rock and roll provides an alternative to classical music, so cult fiction provides an alternative to "high" literature, as cult literature is "from the margins and the extremes." Indeed, of the three books, this one includes the most far-out subjects and obscure titles. It considers cult fiction to be the fiction of the deviant and the socially unacceptable, although the titles it includes are, as they put it, "benign as well as malignant." The authors' selection is decided by "the book, its protagonist and its readers being dislocated in some way from the generally accepted world view of society at large." That is they are outsiders. The authors point out that the readers do not necessarily share the alcoholism, drug or sex addiction of the writers and their books, they may be merely experiencing "the extremes vicariously without ever having to leave our mundane mainstream existence." Calcutt and Shephard suggest that it is in the "uncoded atmosphere [that cult books provide] that human truths are to be found." They certainly give preference in their listings to writers whose lives paralleled their writing. "Dipping their pens in their own blood" is how the authors describe them – William Burroughs, Charles Bukowski,

Kathy Acker and Donald Goines, none of whom I have read, perhaps showing that my own claimed outsiderness is actually only a "mildly on the edge," rather than "completely beyond." Other authors they name are recluses such as Thomas Pynchon and, of course, Salinger. They do point out that cult fiction is a "boy thing," because "women do not have time for such nonsense." Heroes are notably absent in cult fiction and Calcutt and Shephard comment that "cult fiction is the kind of writing young men read at a time when they could no longer harbour great expectations or offer grand actions." They do include the lipogramist Georges Perec, whose eccentricity ran to writing a whole novel without the letter "e" in it. To make up for this, later he wrote *Les Revenentes,* which only used the vowel "e" and none other. Yes, well, women don't usually have time for that I must admit.

*The Rough Guide to Cult Fiction* includes many authors who are neither recluses nor obscure one-book wonders. It is an encyclopedia on the subject and, since most of the authors are still alive, it provides wonderful snippets on the literary gossip scene. Besides bits on cult authors and their books, its sidebars and extras include a list of the most factual cult books, notes on cult characters such as Sherlock Holmes and Holden Caulfield, mention of opium-inspired writers, facts about "what Joseph Stalin did for fiction," and "the Gaddis, Pynchon, Tinasky Mystery" ... well the book is a marvel of information and I've asked my twin to get it for me for Christmas. The introduction states that cult fiction implies lengthy and irrational devotion, although I don't feel you have to be too irrational to love

Nabokov's *Pale Fire,* although you do have to be rather alert to read it. They demand the cult book be out of print for ten years and that the author should "behave abominably in public and die tragically young, or better still, vanish." I am horrified to find that the book claims that the world's first novel is by Xenophon, when I usually claim that position for *The Tales of Genji.*

The third cult fiction book I read was *Classic Cult Fiction.* It starts by quoting Ian Hamilton on *Catcher in the Rye* when he says that that book not only spoke *to* him, but also *for* him. Whissen claims that "when a book has this kind of effect on a sizeable number of readers, then we can say it deserves to be called a 'cult book.'" As he puts it, "reader response rather than author intention," for often the book appears as an ordinary offering and it may be much later that it gets its "cult" label. Cult books do seem to leave the fan with the feeling that the author had them in mind when they wrote the book. However they also plug into the sensibilities of the times in which the book is written.

Some cult books do appeal to only a small section of readers, such as Roch Carrier's *La Guerre, Yes Sir!,* which appealed to anti-war French-Canadians. Whissen puts it that, "breathing a common air, catching light and heat from each other's thoughts, sharing a spirit of general elevation and enlightenment in which all alike communicate – is the essence of the cult fiction experience." Whissen includes elements that cause a book to become a cult book as: an overwhelming admiration by the reader; an isolated, aloof figure as protagonist in the book, which the reader sees as a reflection of his condition; suffering (either real or imaginary) as a theme; a provision for the reader for altering the way they view the world (for example, the works of Castaneda and Lobsang Rampa, Hesse's *Siddhartha* and many more). Whissen makes it clear that by reading cult books one can tune in to the times, the frustrations and aspirations of the people around when the book was written. Read all three of the above books and you will become an immediate authority on cult books, you won't even need to read the cult books themselves, and in some cases that would be a blessing.

## MAN

Christmas is drawing ever closer and I am reminded of the endless witty jokes about how hard it is to buy suitable presents for men – socks, shirts, scarves, golf clubs – a very limited list. This got me to thinking about books about men in general, and fathers and sons in particular, for two such books have just entered my book-box.

The first is Michael Chabon's book *Manhood for Amateurs: The Pleasures and Regrets of a Husband, Father, and Son,* ostensibly on his role as father and his memories of his father, but in reality an excuse to include bits and pieces on subjects in which he is interested, e.g., comic books, the night sky, his wife's suicide attempt and baseball. His best writing is when he actually speaks of his immediate family of four kids, although his essay "Like, Cosmic" was wonderful, the telling of Hurricane Agnes and his family's basement ranks high, and the chapter on writing workshops is so well done. Actually, come to think of it, I seem to have marked equal family and non-family essays as worth rereading, though the family ones I find most appealing, so maybe that is why there seemed to be more of them that I had marked.

His essay on his daughter budding into adolescence shows all the concerns of a father who wants to guard a child from harm and yet allow them wings; the paradox all parents have to face. His essay "Normal Time" clearly illustrates how we can yearn for a time that never existed and never will exist – the time when family life ran totally smoothly. *Manhood for Amateurs* finishes with a wonderful account of his daughter's bat mitzvah at the end of which she is carried around on a chair and everyone is dancing. Mr. Chabon comments, "She tossed and shone like a torch as we carried her around the room. I looked up at her grinning and beautiful and terrified and happy ... this is our life happening, I told her, or would have told her if I could have caught my breath long enough to say it over the clamor of the clarinet and the fiddle, and it's happening right *now*." This is beautiful writing and a picture of a wonderfully involved and concerned father.

Of his early writing years he presents this small gem of a picture, "I would lie in my room feeling alone and friendless and contemplate the ache in me with a distinct sense of anticipatory pleasure, like a child watching his lima bean sprout on a damp paper towel in a dish." About his writing he comments, "My story and my stories are all, in one way or another, the same, tales of solitude and the grand pursuit of connection, of success and the inevitability of defeat." *Time* magazine says of Chabon that he is probably the premier prose stylist – the Updike – of his generation, and the Weekly Standard claims him as the "best writer of English prose in [America]." I loved his *Kavalier & Clay* and while *Manhood for Amateurs* varies in consistency, the weaker pieces just present small troughs to make Chabon's peaks seem even more brilliant.

The second book on fathers and sons (that I mentioned in March) is called just that and is the story of a remarkable family, nine members of which have written one hundred and eight books! The family is the Waughs and the book, *Fathers and Sons: The Autobiography of a Family,* is by Evelyn Waugh's grandson, Alexander Waugh. The problem Alexander Waugh presents is the problem of how to get the fame of his grandfather, Evelyn Waugh, and his father, Auberon Waugh, out of the way so that he could come into his own as a writer. He quoted Ben Johnson in this respect, "Greatness of name in the father often-times overwhelms the son; they stand too near one another. The shadow kills the growth." The problem in the Waugh family was not just that of competing fathers and sons, but also of competing brothers as Evelyn Waugh's books started to outrank those of his brother Alec's (Alexander Raban Waugh). Yes I know the genealogy is getting complicated, but Alexander was the name of Evelyn's brother and also of his grandson whose father, Auberon, also had Alexander as a middle name. If you read the book, you will see a splendid genealogical chart that will put it all straight for you. Still you'll have to go through four hundred and eighty pages and one reader complained that the book was missing 40,364 commas, so be warned.

Alexander's tale of probably the most famous literary family after the Brontës starts in the 1860s with the most disagreeable of the bunch, his great-great-grandfather, Dr. Waugh. Well, they were all pretty disagreeable, whether it was from womanizing, ultra-sharp tongues, alcohol abuse or sexual excesses at public school. As Alexander points out, "to understand how a man behaves as a father it is useful to know how he was treated as a son." For example, Evelyn Waugh's father, Arthur, grossly neglected him in favour of his brother, Alec. Auberon, Alexander's father, commented on this relationship, "sentimentality is the exact measure of a person's inability to experience genuine feeling." Arthur, a publisher and writer himself, was hopelessly sentimental about his eldest son.

Evelyn, the unappreciated son, in turn couldn't wait for his children to return to boarding school after a holiday. He writes, "My news is the great news that all my children have at last disappeared to their various places of education. My unhealthy affection for my second daughter has waned. I now dislike them all equally." Evelyn's comment on children was "of children as of procreation – the pleasure is momentary, the posture ridiculous, the expense damnable."

Evelyn Waugh's novels speak continually of unsuccessful relationships between fathers and sons. Evelyn, in retrospect, seems to many "a bully, a bigot and a snob," but he had the most amazing wit, often stingingly at the expense of others. Auberon, his son, called him "the funniest man of his generation." Alexander's account of this notoriously outspoken family is frank and gossipy. I love the way he constantly says, "I can find no evidence to support that," after he has presented some salacious story, so that in the process, although apparently trying to be fair, he has unintentionally (or maybe intentionally) already done the damage.

Alexander Waugh, as the book draws to its close, comments rather sadly on the human condition saying that "perhaps it is the same for all sons: a childhood of trust (sometimes hero worship) leads to an adolescence of disillusionment and rage." Alexander quotes Maugham on the catharsis that writing provides and he adds that he has now liberated himself from the problems of time (in his book *Time: From Micro-Seconds to Millenia, A Search for the Right Time*), God (in his book *God*) and now fathers and sons in his present writing.

Alexander's father, Auberon, never did anything to court popularity. He said, "Anyone who applies the concept of popular approval to any aspect of his life's philosophy or behaviour is building his house upon a pile of shit." Auberon's tongue was acid and he didn't spare it. He spoke of politics as only suitable for social and emotional misfits; as political columnist for the British magazine *The Spectator* and a constant presence in the parliamentary press gallery, he well knew of what he wrote.

Alexander defines the family of eminent writers by saying, "I suppose, when I think of it, that all of us Waughs, only became writers to impress our fathers." If you have a father interested in books and the lives of irascible writers, Alexander Waugh's *Fathers and Sons* might well find a nice spot under his Christmas tree some year.

# December

Well the Yuletide is upon us and, as the year ends, my thoughts turn to aging in general and my own body in particular. I'm collecting a shelf of books that I can muse on in my old age (although when I'm very old, I'll probably only need one book, for I will have forgotten the beginning by the time I finish it and so can read it time and time again with continued interest). My special shelf contains books I can reread many times without drowsing. *The Globe and Mail* has designated its fifty best books ever, and so can I. Books from the past are very present on my shelf. I'll just mention a few of them, besides my favourite four A. A. Milne classics – no, I didn't have a nanny, but I still think his books reverberate with young children (nanny or not) and, of course, they do with me. The ones I've selected at random are Rumer Godden's *Greengage Summer;* Beverley Nichols' *For Adults Only; The Remains of the Day* by Kazuo Ishiguro; and *84 Charing Cross Road* by Helene Hanff (that had been compared earlier, as I mentioned, to *The Guernsey Literary and Potato Peel Pie Society*).

The first title, *Greengage Summer,* I chose because it is about innocence and experience, about the joys of having a healthy child's integrity and the pains of losing it as hormones churn up. The second, *For Adults Only,* is also about "innocence," since it is a series of small pieces done in drama form, each involving a child asking difficult and often embarrassing questions of an adult. I was just such a child, and this book, even though it's seventy-five years since it was written, still appeals to me with its ability to see life as only an eight-year-old child might.

I simply love *Remains of the Day* even though it is about a rigid caste system and a fascist sympathizer. It is also about a man with a strange loyalty that is rarely heard of these days, a loyalty that refuses to see faults in the person to whom it is faithful, that wears blinkers, which prevent it from seeing any wrongs in that being. It is also a kind of love story, not just the actual unfulfilled one between the butler and the housekeeper, but also the strange love, expressed as loyalty, between servant and master. This world is fast moving towards eradicating such loyalties, and in the story that is exemplified in the butler's relation-ship with a new, American master, towards whom such loyalty would be an alien thing. Ishiguro states, "What I'm interested in is not the actual fact that my characters have done things they later regret ... I'm interested in how they come to terms with it." The butler eventually realizes he has been loyal to a mistaken ideal, and also that by not acting in time, he has lost the possibility of love. Two things very difficult to come to terms with, I should think. It may be a plot spoiler, but the image, at the end of the book, of the butler alone on a seaside pier is one I find extremely moving.

It is the pace of *Remains of the Day,* however, that most seduces me – a time when lawns held croquet hoops and silver was polished regularly. This was a foolish time, I suppose; and my socialist roots are repelled by it, while at the same time my English-conditioning yearns for it.

The last of my selected favourites for my rereading shelf that I'd like to mention is *84 Charing Cross Road*. Again a rather nostalgic book, but this time nostalgic for the era of small, customer-attentive bookstores. The book is made up of letters between an American writer and a noted bookstore, the one demanding books, the other fulfilling orders, and both the demanding and the fulfilling are full of passion – the passion for books, and not just any old books, but for certain editions and particular illustrators. The era of small bookstores is passing and the attention to customers is now provided by Amazon suggesting (by computer algorithms) other titles, similar to the one that you are ordering, that might be to your taste. Sorry, but this just doesn't replace *Charing Cross Road*'s Marks & Co.'s very knowledgeable employee, Frank Doel. Frank was endlessly helpful in supplying books and book suggestions to please the earnest, witty and enthusiastic taste of Helene Hanff. The book is supposedly based on a true story, but whether the letters between Helene and the Marks and Co. employees are the actual letters sent or not, I don't know.

The week before I immigrated to Canada, my then husband and I went to Foyles Bookstore (on the same Charing Cross Road where Marks & Co. was situated), and sold them our complete library. I remember going out for an elegant lunch afterwards with part of the proceeds. Foyles is still managing to hang on, though Marks & Co.

(at 84 Charing Cross Road) has long disappeared. The longing for the time when books were treasured above all things lingers on, however. Anne Bancroft, who wrote the introduction to my edition of *84 Charing Cross Road*, was lucky enough to have a husband, who, realising she had fallen in love with the book, bought the rights so that she could star in the movie.

Helene Hanff's style of letter writing leaves no space between her rich personality and the page and bowls me over with its integrity every time I read the book. My harder-hearted twin pronounces the book "sentimental," but I don't care, for I love this slender volume with intensity and Helene's writing has definitely coloured my own.

Few titles on my favourites shelf coincide with *The Globe and Mail*'s list, but I've reached an age when luckily it doesn't matter to me.

# ΛΙⵏ

December is the time for holiday festivities, but for hostesses it can be a nightmare month. This is the first day in weeks that I can please myself. Last night's dinner party was a success, and the washing and ironing are up-to-date. I click on CBC news, but am not pulled to further explore any of the headlines. I make the bed, play the piano and settle on the couch with an enormous volume of essays by a variety of essayists, from the father of them all, Montaigne, to Annie Dillard and other nature writers. The book is Phillip Lopate's *The Art of the Personal Essay: An Anthology from the Classical Era to the Present.*

Today I have, as Alexander J. Butrim defines it, the leisure of the "meditative mind free to meander leisurely in quiet moments." This doesn't entirely rule out me leaping up occasionally from the couch, in guilt, and doing the odd job, such as washing the kitchen floor. A little housework-grounding stops the mind meandering too far out. Henry James said that "writing was all about seeing the pattern in the carpet," so I feel like a literary cleaning woman as I see a mark on the rug that needs instant attention, which I give it, before returning to the couch.

E. B. White, one of my favourite essayists, claims the essayist is a second-class citizen. I've noticed that this is really a preferred position to be in. Second-class citizens can usually get away with murder, since they are barely noticed – just like the vice-president of anywhere. But I prefer the idea, brought up in Mr. Lopate's book, of the essayist as an accidental philosopher, a person needed at times of transition. Indeed, Joseph Epstein recommends the essay as "the ideal form for ages of transition and uncertain values."

I had decided to write an essay about the essay but found I was inhibited from starting as Phillip Lopate had already done it so brilliantly in his lengthy introduction to *The Art of the Personal Essay.* He speaks of the personal essay as an intimate relationship between the reader and the writer, in which the writer proceeds in an urbane conversational manner and with an unusual level of honesty that at some point reveals more than most people would. As E. B. White says, "There is one thing the essayist cannot do though – he cannot indulge himself in deceit or in concealment, for he will be found out in no time." Phillip Lopate supports this and furthers the function of honesty when he says, "The fulsome confession of limit carries the secret promise of an almost infinite opening-out."

By reading the Lopate book of selected essays, I discover that my copy of Montaigne is lacking the section he wrote on marriage. I, apparently, have the censored version. Montaigne's comments on sexual relations are blunt and witty, and I make a little note on my notepad to add the unexpurgated version to the list of books I send to my two second-hand bookstores in the hopes that, from time to time, they will find some of the titles for me.

ſ∐⊿ſℕ

I know I should be cooking for the upcoming week of dinner parties that I seem to have fixed up for us, but I am still dwelling on the essay, having just read an article by Cristina Nehring on "What's Wrong with the American Essay?" She is specific about the word "American" so maybe I, as a Canadian, still have a chance. Ms. Nehring complains that essay anthologies rot in basements and starts to blame the shortened attention spans of readers for this, then switches, and settles on the cause being that essayists have lost their nerve. Then she moves to also blame editors and compilers of anthologies, as well as authors, for not having the courage to address larger issues.

She finds the essay on modest moments eye-crossingly dull and demands an impassioned analysis of human nature. I lose her at this point, for I find the irritations of the everyday merely a reflection written small of larger injustices. Since the mundane is usually closer to home, I feel it can snag the reader with its familiar resonance (though not apparently Ms. Nehring). I want to remind her of Montaigne's quote, "Every man has within himself the whole human condition." I assume this is true for every woman also.

Ms. Nehring draws a devastating profile of one of those "gentle" essayists she so despises. I could counter with an image of a thoroughly decent, thoughtful, caring individual who prefers consensus to attack, and also prefers small and local to large and impossible. I do not find Montaigne as startling as she does. I find his musings, though admittedly darting here and there, essentially circumnavigate his navel. Not that I don't admire his navel and his remarkable ability to explore and comment on every matter that comes his way. Narcissism can be forgiven if the honesty is startling, I feel. As Alexander Smith wrote of Montaigne, "If you wish to preserve your secret, wrap it up in frankness." I think that Susan Musgrave would give her stamp of approval to that bit of advice, since, as I mentioned earlier, she hides her vulnerability with vulnerability.

Ms. Nehring doesn't want tales, for she demands hypotheses and "muscular maxims" that inspire. She wants the essay to be a "wildcat. Let us give it back its tooth and nail, its fangs and claws." She pleads for the essayist to take risks and pretend they have nine lives. I do not know, nor do I think anybody knows how many lives we have, but I at least know that there are other ways to take on issues besides clawing them to death.

/l◢l\

As contrast to the big, bold themes demanded by Ms. Nehring, I've just been bowled over by Jun'ichirō Tanizaki's brief, lovely book on the small theme of shadows, *In Praise of Shadows*.

Elizabeth Bowen said that "one can live in the shadow of an idea without grasping it" and that, I'm afraid defines my reading of most of the non-fiction science books that frequent our house. Still the shadow seems to be enough for me as I read endlessly of endless universes and of branes and quarks and anti-matter and other such fascinating ideas. "Science," Stewart Brand is quoted as saying, "is the only news; all else is hearsay and gossip." The history of science, with its blockings of up-and-coming young scientists and the sidelining of others by jealousy, might indicate that science does not meet such pleasant claims as Mr. Brand thinks it does, but it tries.

Shadows have always appealed to me, and if my understanding of science is but "a shadow of an idea," then that will have to do for the while. When Jerome K. Jerome said, "Time is but the shadow of the world upon the background of Eternity," whatever that might mean, he probably was just as enchanted, and just as ignorant about the mysteries of the universe as I am.

Shadows have been a thread running through my life. Twilight is my favourite time of day and the image of long shadows in the autumn twilight beats anything else I know for stark loneliness and the sadness of the ways of men (and women). From Dostoevsky's wonderful image of "the shadow of a coachman rubbing the shadow of a coach with the shadow of a brush," (spoken, I believe, by Alyosha's father in *The Brothers Karamazov*) to Jun'ichirō Tanizaki's brilliant essay on shadows, all mentions encourage my own use of shadows in my poetry.

...
loneliness, loneliness, loneliness,
where skin divides
and even your face in the mirror
will not reply to your
endless questions, and
your shadow, when approached,
turns slightly away.

Tanizaki, a Japanese novelist, who lived from 1886 to 1965, expounds on the importance of shadows in Japanese life in this novella-length essay, from the deep eaves that make the interiors of Japanese rooms dark, to the appreciation of shadow on Japanese art objects. When talking about beauty, he says, "The quality that we call beauty, however, must always grow from the realities of life, and our ancestors, forced to live in dark rooms, because of the deep overhang of the roof, presently came to discover beauty in shadows, ultimately to guide shadows towards beauty's ends." Tanizaki suggested that Easterners accept things as they are more than Westerners, "we resign ourselves to it as inevitable. If light is scarce then light is scarce; we will immerse ourselves in the darkness and there discover its own particular beauty." He adds, "We [Easterners] find beauty not only in the thing itself, but in the pattern of shadows, the light and darkness, which that thing provides."

The other day, instead of glancing into my husband's studio as I usually do as I come up the basement stairs, I entered the room, and suddenly I was confronted with a troop of his sculptures almost trapping me. What was startling was the incredible shadow-play of the elements of his constructions. It was almost as though they had come alive and were shimmering. Eli's sculptures are strong on form and very architectural. They provide ample patterns of light and darkness. Tanizaki would have appreciated them.

My love of shadows was evidenced even in my childhood when the poem by Robert Louis Stevenson beginning "I have a little shadow that goes in and out with me ..." haunted me, as I sought alternative company to my ever-present twin sister in my often present shadow. Even when it comes to something as mundane as golf, Sam Snead's quote, "These greens are so fast I have to hold my putter over the ball and hit it with the shadow," holds me with its fascinating image.

Of course we all know that Plato defined our experience of the "real" world as shadows. He compares our lives to those of cave dwellers in a cave lit by a small fire. The fire, situated behind them, projects the shadows of the real world on to the caves walls, and that is all they (and, by inference, we) are able to see. And Blake's "imagination is the real and eternal world of which this vegetable universe is but a faint shadow" somehow echoes Plato's ideas.

I think Tanizaki would have appreciated these quotes for his Japanese sensibilities, so well displayed in *In Praise of Shadows,* would have immediately resonated with their perceptions.

### ⅠⅬⅣⅠⅥ

There is nothing shadowy about the possible purchase, about this time of year, of coffee-table books; books to impress the recipient by their size, weight and price. Two have just threatened to sag the legs of my second-hand faux-oak coffee table. The first is *Vanity Fair: The Portraits: A Century of Iconic Images* and is just what it says, hundreds of portraits from the pages of the magazine *Vanity Fair. Vanity Fair* ran from 1913-1936 and then was revived in 1983 by the same founding firm of Condé Nast. The full-page photographs in this giant book, by many well-known photographers, present you with most of the icons of the twentieth century. To add to the appeal of this book are three excellent essays: one by Christopher Hitchens, which gives a general history of the life and times of the magazine; one by Terence Pepper, "The Portrait Photograph in the Modern Age;" and one by David Friend on the recent years called "*Vanity Fair,* 1983-Now: A New Magazine for a New Age." I live a life far from those of the notables photographed in these pages (I have only seen two in the flesh – Johnny Weissmuller, the original

Tarzan in the first talkies, and Martina Navratilova, the tennis star), and yet I am weeping and laughing at these portraits as if they were part of my own family album. I am not a pack rat, having few photographs of my past – only one of my second wedding and few of Eli and my years of travels, so it is lucky that these large and quite wonderful photos help me recall some of the lands in which I have lived and travelled, and some of the books I have read and films I have seen. Paul Robeson's powerful image by Edward Steichen; Charlie Chaplin's shy, meditative and handsome face, captured by Baron de Meyer; and George Gershwin's portrait – again by Steichen are some of my favourites from the book. There were few prominent writers who didn't write for the early editions of *Vanity Fair* and today, apparently, they can call on writers of equal standing.

The first editor of Vanity Fair, Frank Crowninshield, stated his purpose was to "take a dozen or so cultivated men and women; dress them becomingly; sit them down to dinner." He would then ask, "What will these people say?" I suspect my provincialism (and deafness) would prevent me fully participating in such a gathering. I have never opened a copy of the magazine, but the book, *Vanity Fair: The Portraits,* fascinates and horrifies me. It fascinates with the brilliance of the photographic art and horrifies me to find that the whole of our North American culture, and all these years of so-called civilization, are dominated by so many Hollywood starlets.

Be warned, the seventy-two dollars you have to put out for this book does not guarantee that the spine will not totally break down as this copy's spine appears to have done on page one hundred ninety-two.

The other coffee-table book I have for Christmas perusal is a serious tome on architectural excellence called just that, *Architectural Excellence: In a Diverse World Culture.* It is by the Atlanta architect, William T. Baker, and it selects many of the finest buildings in man's history to illustrate his thesis that great architecture exemplifies five principles. These are that the architecture: should have continuity with tradition; should have a rational basis; should allow for Nature's scale (rhythm, proportion, symmetry, etc.); its form should be based on function and it should choose its material wisely. Since the book covers architecture in many different lands and various traditions, Baker feels that, in addition to his principles, good architecture should adhere to regional forms and have culturally significant ornament.

I yellow-tab the structures that most appeal to me and then sit and meditate on what buildings as disparate as the Olympic Stadium in Beijing, the Shaker Round barn and the earliest un-restored church in Ireland might have in common for me. I come to the conclusion that, like my husband, I love the repetition of units, the symmetry of the Shaker buildings and the integrity of form and function of such buildings as Moshe Safdie's Habitat '67 in Montreal, and Corbusier's church, Notre Dame du Haut, in Ronchamp, France. An occasional choice, such as the carnival of St. Basil's Cathedral on Red Square in Moscow, provides a note of frivolity in my taste, but mostly I go for buildings which have a *wabi-sabi* touch to them. I also appreciate buildings that blend in with the landscape, such as Renzo Piano's fabulous tribute building to Jean-Marie Tjibaou in New Caledonia.

I add to my selection a few buildings that have a certain simplicity, yet reflect a wealth of humanity within, such as Carl Larsson's house in Sundborn. Our small vinyl-sided cottage on Gabriola exhibits none of Baker's principles, yet inside, the reuse of others' castaways and the objects of our own creativity, luckily overshadow the wall-to-wall non-wool carpet and the lino flooring of the kitchen and dining area. The transmutation of shoddy to joyful is a principle of mine that Baker may well have over-looked. I love books that stimulate me to stretch my imagination and both *Vanity Fair: The Portraits* and *Architectural Excellence: In a Diverse World Culture* have just filled the bill.

## ⅍⅄

After a year of intense and ferocious reading, I have come upon a modest sixty-four page book that just about sums things up for me when it comes to "reading" and "writing." It is, in fact, just called *Reading and Writing,* and is by the eminent Canadian writer, Robertson Davies. When I describe the book as modest I am merely referring to the size, for Mr. Davies is here very present and larger than life (and he was large in life), and he comes through as a rather pompous and opinionated person. I agreed with many of the opinions he laid out in this book, but disagreed rather firmly with one in particular. Davies was not afraid to make sweeping statements and take unpopular positions. He was computer-illiterate, saying, "I don't want a word-processor. I process my own words." I'm pretty sure he would have changed that position had he lived into the twenty-first century.

Robertson Davies advocated reading not just for personal pleasure but for personal exploration. He despised the mediocre, but didn't demand people only read the best. He felt mediocre books were a worse influence than reading downright trash. He doesn't elaborate on this, but it certainly raises questions. Reviewers he also despised, pointing out that "reviews are written often in great haste, to establish the reputations of the reviewer, rather than to give a careful assessment of what an author has worked very hard to make as good as he can." I just must include here the very relevant quote Davies gives by Thornton Wilder about writers, "A writer should certainly read criticism of his work and give it adequate but not prolonged consideration, or else he would find that the critic has wormed into his mind and was writing his next book."

Davies recommends slow, thorough reading, pointing out that "you are trying to find out what the book has to say. You are not straining to reach the end, in order that you may read something else." As I am promoting readership as a serious occupation, I thoroughly endorse Davies' opinion that "literature is an art, and reading is also an art, and unless you recognize and develop your qualities as an interpretive artist you are not getting the best from your reading."

I love his quote from John Middleton Murray, "A truly great novel is a tale to the simple, a parable to the wise, and a direct revelation of reality to the man who has made it a part of his being." I also like Davies' devastating negativity towards grants. "Nothing – including grants – is for nothing," he warns, and reminds us that Robert Graves said that "a poet who writes for money will be rejected by the White Goddess from whom all poetic inspiration comes."

He pounds reductive criticism by paralleling reading to looking at a clock, "If you observe it understandingly it will tell you what time it is in my life and yours, but if you pull it apart you will have nothing but a handful of junk." He believes that the writer is telling the reader things that they already know but have not yet recognized that they do. The ability to do this Davies calls *"shamnstvo,"* a Russian word meaning enchantment. This is enchanting writing and I recognise that I already knew all the things he is telling me in *Reading and Writing,* but just hadn't got them down on paper yet. If you are an avid reader, this may well be the best sixty-four pages you will ever read on the subject of reading and writing.

Mr. Davies and I firmly disagreed when he states, "The worst thing that can happen to a writer is to draw upon himself in his work until he knows nobody except other writers; he is then reduced to the literary desperation of writing a book about a man who is writing a book, and when he does that we know he is finished." I am fast approaching being such a writer but I feel neither barren nor desperate. I have experienced enough junk and beauty in my seventy-eight years to fill endless books, so why shouldn't I delve into my own being as a source of inspiration, Mr. Davies? Still Robertson Davies is a wonderful advocate for reading and, in addition, he has read Proust's tome several times, so he gets extra points for that.

**⫼⊿⫯**

Well, it may be a strange way to spend the holiday period, but I have recently acquired Lawrence Durrell's Alexandria Quartet (*Justine, Balthazar, Mountolive* and *Cleo*) from our recycling depot and intend to spend the holidays revisiting them. My twin informs me on the phone from London that I will be disappointed in them, so we'll see. I just revisited Maugham's *Cakes and Ale* and am sure I got more out of it this time then on my original reading. *Cakes and Ale* is so funny, and still so relevant with its caustic picture of writers and the publishing world; a world in which writers become famous because critics, or pop stars, choose to read them, and authors are considered notable because of the selfsame critics promotion, along with academia adding its two halfpence worth.

Back to Lawrence Durrell, I am noting quotes and have started with "Humility! The last trap that awaits the ego in search of absolute truth." Mr. Durrell later modifies his demand for the absolute truth with the quote, "We are all hunting for rational reasons for believing in the absurd."

I did love Durrell's quote in *Balthazar* where he says, "We are all racing under sealed handicaps." Another one of his quotes, "Science is the poetry of the intellect and poetry the science of the heart's affections," I just adore, although I haven't the slightest idea what it means.

I'm thinking of my years of meditation for some reason, I suppose because the solstice is a good time for contemplation of things like good and evil, and why there is something instead of nothing. Lawrence Durrell, whose books are occupying most of my thoughts these days, thinks that sin is anything that is pressed too far.

Durrell certainly dwells on love in his four volumes, perhaps not to the point of sinfulness though. His characters sit around analysing it, shifting it around like disconsolate children. Even when lovemaking, or at least going through the motions, they think and talk of aspects of love that have never even come within a mile of my insensitive brain. Lawrence Durrell was overshadowed by his more-famous brother, Gerald – the collector of animals. Gerald presents Lawrence as pompous and self-important in his fun book, *My Family and Other Animals,* but Lawrence was a fine writer in his own field and doesn't need to be compared with his brother, though folks always will. The Alexandria Quartet put him on centre stage. My twin was entirely wrong, because although Lawrence Durrell is almost unknown today (our little-island librarian and I have founded his Gabriola fan club, and are its sole members at the moment), I became totally absorbed in the world he had created and my holiday anxieties moved to a back burner.

Well, The Alexandria Quartet is behind me. From the four books I have gathered a couple of things that might help me in the New Year. Lawrence Durrell recommends that for "those of us who feel deeply and who are at all conscious of the inextricable tangle of human thoughts there is only one response to be made – ironic tenderness and silence." He gives two, although he had said one, but I am not complaining. To these two I add Michael Faraday's advice, "Work. Finish. Publish," to my New Year's resolutions' list. But what if your "work" is piled in a mess of papers on your desk? Who said "it's not the tragedies that kill us, it's the messes"? Dorothy Parker? Well, who else could it be? I'll finish the year on this cheerful, though somewhat cynical, note.

# Afterword

That was an intense year of reading. I covered the old, the new, the borrowed and books singing the blues. I do somewhat feel like a bride as I once again renew my vows to the written word – to love and promote it, to trumpet widely of its importance and significance in a damaged world.

Our local library system is asking its readers to record the number of books they read over a certain period. The library with the most books read per head gets some kind of reward – maybe faster indexing of new books by the crew at headquarters, or maybe higher pay for our wonderful Gabriola Island desk clerks who know our needs almost as intimately as we do ourselves. I take some pride in upping our library's record since I've probably read at least four books a week this year. My husband may have taken out many more, but they linger in his fruit-crate storage box, for he is a much slower reader than I.

Has the reading changed me? you may ask anxiously, worried about my hours devoted to turning pages and the state of my eyesight. Ammon Shea, the man who spent a year reading the twenty-three thousand pages of the *Oxford English Dictionary*, needed glasses by the end of the year and was luckily diverted, by the arrival of his first child, from repeating the experiment the following year as he was tempted to do. I am going for an eye checkup in January, but the state of my being, which concerns me a little more, is robust. Reading books, whether great or less than great, has confirmed my resolution to continue reading avidly and writing obsessively. My reading has also confirmed my role as creative reader. This is the type of reader who brings their all to a book, in respect for the many hours (and often years) put in by the author. These readers have great expectations from the book, expectations that they will be spun around by it and whisked to the ends of the universe. Or, more modestly, such readers expect, at least that books should give them the inspiration that will allow them to live yet one more day with some kind of creative intensity, and always, always with a degree of hope.

> when reading
> even in fiction I search
> for "how-to"
> how to live more fully
> how to bite into an autumn fruit

# A Reader's Bibliography

*84 Charing Cross Road,* Helene Hanff

*180 More: Extraordinary Poems for Every day,* Billy Collins

*1001 Books You Must Read Before You Die,* ed. Peter Boxall

*A. A. Milne,* Ann Thwaite

Alexandria Quartet (*Justine, Balthazar, Mountolive* and *Cleo*), Lawrence Durrell

*The Amazing Adventures of Kavalier & Clay,* Michael Chabon

*Archy and Mehitabel,* Don Marquis

*Architectural Excellence: In a Diverse World Culture,* William T. Baker

*The Art of the Gaman: Arts and Crafts from the Japanese American Internment Camps 1942-1946,* Delphine Hirasuna, Kit Hinrichs and Terry Heffernan

*The Art of the Personal Essay: An Anthology from the Classical Era to the Present,* Phillip Lapote

*The Autobiography of Alice B. Toklas,* Gertrude Stein

*Balzac and the Little Chinese Seamstress,* Dai Sijie

*Barefoot Gen,* Keiji Nakazawa

*Bitter Fame: A Life of Sylvia Plath,* Anne Stevenson

*The Book of Negroes,* Lawrence Hill

*The Book of Numbers: The Secret of Numbers and How They Changed the World,* Peter J. Bentley

*The Book of Sand,* Jorge Luis Borges

*The Botany of Desire: A Plant's-Eye View of the World,* Michael Pollan

*The Brontës,* Juliet Barker

*Business in Eden,* David Cobb

*Cake or Death: The Excruciating Choices of Everyday Life,* Heather Mallick

*Cakes and Ale,* William Somerset Maugham

*Captain Corelli's Mandolin,* Louis de Bernières

*Classic Cult Fiction: A Companion to Popular Cult Literature,* Thomas Reed Whissen

*Cloud Atlas,* David Mitchell

*The Comedy of Survival: Literary Ecology and a Play Ethic,* Joseph W. Meeker

*The Compact Culture: The Japanese Tradition of "Smaller Is Better,"* O-Young Lee

*Crazy About Gardening: Humorous Reflections on the Sweet Seductions of a Garden,* Des Kennedy

*Crow Boy,* Taro Yashima

*Cult Fiction: A Reader's Guide,* Andrew Calcutt and Richard Shephard

*Curious Pursuits: Occasional Writing,* Margaret Atwood

*D. H. Lawrence: The Life of an Outsider,* John Worthen

*Deluxe: How Luxury Lost Its Luster,* Dana Thomas

*The Diving Bell and the Butterfly,* Jean-Dominique Bauby

*Doctor Faustus,* Thomas Mann

*The Din in the Head,* Cynthia Ozick

*Dragonhunt,* Frances (Sandy) Duncan

*The Enchanted Places,* Christopher Robin Milne

*Ethel & Ernest: A True Story*, Raymond Briggs

*Ex Libris: Confessions of a Common Reader*, Anne Fadiman

*Fathers and Sons: The Autobiography of a Family*, Alexander Waugh

*The Final Solution: A Story of Detection*, Michael Chabon

*Flower Confidential: The Good, the Bad, and the Beautiful*, Amy Stewart

*For Adults Only*, Beverley Nichols

*For the Relief of Unbearable Urges*, Nathan Englander

*French Dirt: The Story of a Garden in the South of France*, Richard Goodman

*From Man to Man*, Moishe Nadir

*The Garden in Winter*, Rosemary Verey

*Garden Voices: Two Centuries of Canadian Garden Writing*, ed. Edwinna von Baeyer and Pleasance Crawford

*The Gardener's Year*, Karel Čapek

*Greengage Summer*, Rumer Godden

*Green Thoughts: A Writer in the Garden*, Eleanor Perényi

*The Guernsey Literary and Potato Peel Society*, Mary Ann Shaffer and Annie Barrows

*A History of Britain: At the Edge of the World? 3000 BC – AD 1603*, Simon Schama

*History of the Conquest of Peru*, William Hickling Prescott

*History of the Conquest of Mexico*, William Hickling Prescott

*Hollow on the Hill: The Search for a Personal Philosophy*, Christopher Robin Milne

*Home Before Dark: A Personal Memoir of John Cheever by his Daughter*, Susan Cheever

*How to Read and Why*, Harold Bloom

*How to Talk About Books You Haven't Read,* Pierre Bayard

*I am a Cat,* Sōseki Natsume

*In Bed with the Word: Reading, Spirituality, and Cultural Politics,* Daniel Coleman

*In Praise of Shadows,* Jun'ichirō Tanizaki

*In The Freud Archives,* Janet Malcolm

*The Kagero Diary: A Woman's Autobiographical Text from Tenth-Century Japan,* trans. Sonja Arntzen

*Kwaidan: stories and studies of strange things,* Lafcadio Hearn

*Lady Chatterley's Lover,* D. H. Lawrence

*Lark Rise,* Flora Thompson

*Last Lovers,* William Wharton

*Lavengro: The Scholar, the Gypsy, the Priest,* George Borrow

*The Life of D. H. Lawrence,* Keith Sagar

*The Literary Works of Ou-yang Hsiu (1007-72),* Ronald C. Egan

*The Little Drummer Girl,* John le Carré

*Love That Dog,* Sharon Creech

*Madame Bovary's Ovaries: A Darwinian Look at Literature,* David and Nanelle Barash

*The Man Who Made Lists: Love, Death, Madness, and the Creation of "Roget's Thesaurus,"* Joshua Kendall

*The Man who Planted Trees,* Jean Giono, trans. Peter Doyle

*Manhood for Amateurs: The Pleasures and Regrets of a Husband, Father, and Son,* Michael Chabon

*Maps and Legends: Reading and Writing Along the Borderlands,* Michael Chabon

*Marginalia: Readers Writing in Books,* H. J. Jackson

*The Mating Mind: How Sexual Choice Shaped the Evolution of Human Nature*, Geoffrey Miller

*Maus*, Art Spiegelman

*Ming Lo Moves the Mountain*, Arnold Lobel

*The Ministry of Special Cases*, Nathan Englander

*Miss Leavitt's Stars: The Untold Story of the Woman Who Discovered How to Measure the Universe*, George Johnson

*Music of the Primes: Searching to Solve the Greatest Mystery in Mathematics*, Marcus du Sautoy

*My Garden (Book)*, Jamaica Kincaid

*Nothing to be Frightened Of*, Julian Barnes

*Oak and Company*, Richard Mabey

*The Ode Less Travelled: Unlocking the Poet Within*, Stephen Fry

*On Being Certain: Believing You Are Right Even When You're Not*, Robert A. Burton

*The Path Through the Trees*, Christopher Robin Milne

*Pearls in Vinegar: The Pillow Book of Heather Mallick*, Heather Mallick

*Poetry 180: a turning back to poetry*, ed. Billy Collins

*The Rainbow*, D. H. Lawrence

*Reading and Writing*, Robertson Davies

*Reading Like a Writer: A Guide for People Who Love Books and for Those Who Want to Write Them*, Francine Prose

*The Remains of the Day*, Kazuo Ishiguro

*The Rest is Noise: Listening to the Twentieth Century*, Alex Ross

*The Rough Guide to Cult Fiction*, ed. Paul Simpson, Michaela Bushell and Helen Rodiss

*Second Nature: A Gardener's Education*, Michael Pollan

*A Shortcut Through Time: The Path to the Quantum Computer,* George Johnson

*The Silent Woman: Sylvia Plath and Ted Hughes,* Janet Malcolm

*The Stuff of Thought: Language as a Window into Human Nature,* Steven Pinker

*Suite Française,* Irène Némirovsky

*The Tale of Genji,* Murasaki Shikibu, trans. Royall Tyler

*The Taoist Priest of Laoshan Mountain,* Cao Zuorui

*The Ten Most Beautiful Experiments,* George Johnson

*Two Lives: Gertrude and Alice,* Janet Malcolm

*The Uncommon Reader,* Alan Bennett

*The Uses and Abuses of History,* Margaret MacMillan

*Vanity Fair: The Portraits: A Century of Iconic Images,* Graydon Carter and David Friend

*The View from Castle Rock,* Alice Munro

*The Virgin and the Gypsy,* D. H. Lawrence

*Walden,* Henry David Thoreau

*The Wapshot Scandal,* John Cheever

*Waterlog,* Roger Deakin

*The Well-Tempered Garden,* Christopher Lloyd

*What do Authors Do?,* Eileen Christelow

*When You are Engulfed in Flames,* David Sedaris

*The Whole Five Feet: What the Great Books Taught Me About Life, Death, And Pretty Much Everything Else,* Christopher Beha

*Why Read?,* Mark Edmundson

*Women in Love,* D. H. Lawrence

*Writing Life: Celebrated Canadian and International Authors on Writing and Life,* ed. Constance Rooke

Naomi Beth Wakan has written over thirty books including *Images of Japan, Segues, Compositions: Notes on the written word* and *Late Bloomer: On Writing Later in Life.* Her book *Haiku – one breath poetry* was an American Library Association selection. Her essays, haiku and tanka have appeared in many magazines and anthologies and have been broadcasted on the CBC. Naomi lives on Gabiola Island with her husband, the sculptor, Elias Wakan.